Advance Praise

"I have known Mark for years, and he is one of those people who don't just talk the talk in real estate, but walk the walk."

—JOE FAIRLESS, HOST OF THE *BEST EVER REAL ESTATE INVESTING ADVICE* PODCAST

"When it comes to passive income without headaches, there are only a few people I recommend, and Mark is one of them."

—ARI MEISEL, AUTHOR OF *LESS DOING, MORE LIVING*

"If Mark Podolsky didn't exist, we'd need to invent him to make our real estate lives easier."

—KEITH WEINHOLD, FOUNDER AND OWNER, GET RICH EDUCATION

"As a professional real estate investor, it always amazes me how many different ways there are to make money. It's also critical for all investors to find ways not to just "do deals," but to generate passive income, as it's a critical resource to what we're all looking for: income while we sleep. Dirt Rich is a refreshing and exciting perspective on how to create passive income without having to deal with tenants, termites, or many of the other headaches typical of traditional 'passive' investments."

—MIKE HAMBRIGHT, CHIEF NERD, FLIPNERD.COM

"My friend Mark Podolsky is master at one of the most over-looked and easiest strategies for making a lot of money with real estate. In Dirt Rich, Mark reveals the strategy that he used to go from broke to millionaire, but it doesn't stop there. He not only outlines the steps that you can take to start with a little bit of money and create cash flow from buying and selling land, but in his story you'll also find the keys to a happy and fulfilling life."

—JOANNE MUSA, THE TAX LIEN LADY, BEST-SELLING AUTHOR OF *TAX LIEN INVESTING SECRETS: HOW YOU CAN GET 8%–36% RETURN ON YOUR MONEY WITHOUT THE TYPICAL RISK OF REAL ESTATE OR THE UNCERTAINTY OF THE STOCK MARKET*

"I have known Mark for years, and he is a true pioneer with a wealth of knowledge to share about the niche of land investing."

—SETH WILLIAMS, RETIPSTER.COM

"No smoke, no fluff, this is the raw, honest, and totally doable way to go from dirt poor to dirt rich in land investing from the guy who grew wealth from the ground up. What's rare in the guru world is finding a guy like Mark who does what he teaches and makes as much money in the business as teaching the business. I trust Mark and his integrity and highly recommend this book to anyone—either starting out or deep into real estate investing—for a strategy I wish I'd started with before I bought 150 houses and had tenants coming out my ears."

—DAMION LUPO, CCIM, AUTHOR OF *THE QUICK & DIRTY GUIDE TO THE QRP* AND *BLACK BELT WEALTH*

Dirt Rich

Dirt Rich

How One Ambitiously Lazy
Geek Created Passive Income
in Real Estate without Renters,
Renovations, and Rehabs

Mark Podolsky

LIONCREST
PUBLISHING

DIRT RICH
How One Ambitiously Lazy Geek Created Passive Income in Real Estate without Renters, Renovations, and Rehabs

ISBN   978-1-5445-1077-4 *Paperback*
       978-1-5445-1076-7 *Ebook*

Contents

Claim Your Free Additional Training

In this book, you're going to learn how to create a passive income in real estate investing without the typical headaches like tenants, toilets, termites, and trash.

As you're reading the book, if you want to start implementing the foundational elements and "earn and learn," please register for our $97 wholesaling course for FREE.

This course will teach you how to double your money in 30 days or less so you can start building your cash reserves to acquire more raw land and start building your passive income.

See you on the other side: http://www.thelandgeek.com/quickdeals

Why I Hate
Business Books

———

I love apps such as Blinkist and Hardbound that take business books and extract all the best ideas. Almost every
business book I've read has a simple concept explained
in the first fifteen pages, and then the other 250 pages are
anecdotes, science, and other extraneous information to
hammer the point home to the reader.

If you don't want to read this book in its entirety and want
the quick blink, here it is: you have a story, and you can
change that story. Solo economic dependency means
if you aren't working, you aren't making any money.
It's not good. Get out of solo economic dependency by
doing this: buy assets pennies on the dollar. Sell those
assets on a subscription basis for passive income. Repeat
ad infinitum.

There you go! The whole book in a few sentences. If you'd like to read further, my wish for you is for your mind to open up to the possibilities of land investing and how it can improve your life on every level—more time, more money, and more freedom. I also don't want you to make the same dumb mistakes I did personally and professionally, so it's all laid out below.

I hope to see you on the other side.

To engineering your success,

MARK J. PODOLSKY

a.k.a. the Land Geek

Chapter 1

Birth of a Land Geek

——

Suppose making a lot of money is your goal and suppose you make enough so that making more has no marginal utility. Then it would be foolish to continue to have making money be your goal. People who acquire things beyond their usefulness not only will derive little or no marginal gains from these acquisitions, but they also will experience negative consequences, as with any form of gluttony. So, because of the law of diminishing returns, it is only natural that seeking something new, or seeking new depths of something old, is required to bring us satisfaction.

—RAY DALIO, BRIDGEWATER HEDGE FUND

How Much Is Enough? A Parable

The American businessman was at the pier of a small coastal Mexican village when a small boat with just one fisherman docked. In the bottom of the small boat were several large yellowfin tuna. The businessman complimented the Mexican on the quality of his fish and asked how long it took to catch them. The Mexican replied, "Only a little while, senor."

"So why don't you stay out longer and catch more fish?" the businessman asked.

"I earn enough to cover my family's immediate needs," answered the fisherman, shrugging.

"But what do you do with the rest of your time?"

The fisherman answered, "I sleep late, fish a little, play with my children, take a siesta with my wife, Maria, stroll into the village each evening where I sip wine and play guitar with my amigos. I have a full and busy life, senor."

The American scoffed. "I am a Harvard MBA, and I could help you. You should spend more time fishing and with the proceeds buy a bigger boat. With the proceeds from the bigger boat you could buy several boats; eventually, you would have a fleet of fishing boats. Instead of selling your catch to a middleman, you would sell directly to the processor and, in time, open your own cannery. You would control the product, processing, and distribution. You would need to leave this small village and move to Mexico City, then Los Angeles, and eventually New York City where you would run your expanding enterprise."

The Mexican fisherman asked, "But senor, how long will this all take?"

"Fifteen to twenty years."

"So long? But what then, senor?"

The businessman laughed and said, "That's the best part! When the time is right, you would announce an IPO and sell your company stock to the public and become very rich. You would make millions of dollars."

"Millions, senor? Then what?"

"Then you would retire, of course. Move to a small coastal fishing village where you would sleep late, fish a little, play with your grandkids, take a siesta with your wife, stroll to the village in the evenings where you could sip wine and play your guitar with your amigos."

The fisherman just smiled. "Good day, senor." Tipping his straw hat politely to the American visitor, he strolled away into the village.

The businessman shuddered, the shards of the glass

bubble in which he had encased himself shattering all around. The folly of what he had just been saying became clear, his own miserable life reflected with nauseating clarity in the fisherman's eyes. In one life-changing moment, he realized how miserable he really was and how much he dreaded going back to work. He laughed uncontrollably until the tears ran down his cheeks. Shaking his head, he went back to his hotel. The next day, he flew home and quit his high-stress, sixty-hour-a-week job.

Much of our lives are spent in the elusive quest for money. We want more, more, and then more. Dollars lose their meaning. Once we have enough, they eventually become nothing but an addictive video game. Dollars aren't an end in themselves. You can be successful as long as you bring in *enough* money to continue your business and be able to do what you want to do in life.

How I Became a Hungry Ghost: Parkinson's Law of Money

It was 2010, and in a year and a half, I had gone from a comfortable six-figure income and a lavish lifestyle to having to short-sell my house and sell my car to make ends meet. To say my ego was crushed was an understatement. I felt like a total failure—a poor provider, a selfish husband, and a father who had let his children down in the most dramatic way possible. One night, back at our modest rental home at around 1:00 a.m. after staying out late drinking with a buddy and feeling horrible about my circumstances, I had a panic attack, passed out, and cut my chin when I collapsed. I remember thinking right before I passed out how badly I had disappointed my kids. Then I screamed to my wife and hit the floor. She took me to the hospital. I was lucky I didn't really hurt myself on the way down or when I landed. And if I'd been fifteen years older and not in excellent physical shape, it could have been a heart attack instead of a panic attack, and I might not be here to tell you this story.

Looking back, I realize that over the five years or so before my crisis, my wife and I had been slowly turning into what Chinese Buddhists call hungry ghosts while still alive. Some people, in this Chinese tradition, become hungry ghosts after they die because they were ungenerous and refused to share with those in need, others because they were simply greedy and avaricious. One type of hungry ghost has a mouth in which all food and drink becomes fire and burns them. Another has a pinhole mouth, so that it can never get enough to eat. We had forgotten how much was enough, so what we had was never enough.

Every happiness study states that after around $75K in income, our happiness only marginally increases up to $250K. After $250K, more money will not increase happiness and in some cases can actually cause unhappiness. So the question I often ask myself is, "How much is enough?" The answer, I think, for most people anyway, is $10K/month in passive income. Ideally, $20K/month in passive income would be the ultimate goal, but that $10K/month will get most people completely free to work when they want, with whom they want, and where they want.

Unfortunately, I forgot about that a few years back.

My Story

But it's easy to see how it can happen. Flash back to 2001. I'm on a treadmill of misery and exhaustion at a job I hate. My wife and I have a six-month-old baby boy. We're living paycheck to paycheck and can't even make ends meet. And we're having one of our most frequent arguments. My wife wants to buy organic baby food, but I've been looking at the pennies in the bank account and I can't justify the extra cost. Does this kind of marital conflict sound familiar? I can't say that any one of these fights, or being perpetually almost broke, or the wretchedness of my job was what cemented my determination to create a new kind of life for me and my family.

As you might guess from what I've just told you, I didn't grow up rich. My father worked as a wholesale grocer, and my mother was a legal secretary. I grew up the same way so many middle-class kids do. My father was a bit of a workaholic, and I didn't see him much as a kid except on weekends. My mom struggled to raise my sister and me like a single mother, except that she had my dad's income. And both of them told us, "Get a good education, and get a good job." And you know what? I did—the education part anyway. I graduated from Indiana University and was planning to go to law school.

However, I got the travel bug and moved to Australia for six months instead of going to law school. Like most brooding young men, I was trying to figure out what I wanted to do with my life. So then I just bounced around from job to job until I met my wife and moved to Arizona.

As a newlywed, I became an investment banker working with private equity groups in mergers and acquisitions—a high-pressure, small salary, basically a commission-only job. My work was to cold-call business owners and somehow miraculously convince them to let me sell their business or represent them in buying a business, despite having no knowledge of their company. Needless to say, constant rejection was a way of life.

To make matters worse, I had a forty-five-minute commute to work there and back. I had an overbearing boss who would second-guess every decision I made and every action I took. He loved to micromanage me every minute of every day. So each morning, as I was jolted awake by my buzzing alarm clock, I'd feel violently ill at the thought of going to work. This job was sucking the life out of me, crushing my soul, and destroying my confidence. Some days I'd go home after work and not even have the energy to speak to my wife. I'd be so run-down that she would almost have to force me to eat dinner rather than go directly to bed.

I was fed up with a work environment that was based on lies, politics, and ass-kissing. It made me feel dirty, because if I wanted to get ahead and really succeed as an investment banker, I would have to surrender my integrity and personal values.

No matter how hard I worked, at the end of the day I had no control over my income.

Birth of a Land Geek

Fate intervened one day when my firm hired a new banker who was working a side hustle of land flipping. We had a beer together, and he told me how he was making money hand over fist buying land at county tax-foreclosure auctions. I was amazed by what he was telling me, so I wrote down his secrets on a bar napkin and said to myself, "This could be it."

So I began looking into it seriously. If anything, I hated

my job even more because I wasn't getting enough sleep. But I felt better about my life already because I had a goal beyond getting through the next day, the next week, the next month, to the next paycheck. Finally, after many late nights researching, reading articles online, and reading various books borrowed from the local library, it was time for me to take action.

I remember my first auction in New Mexico like it was yesterday. I was a nervous wreck. My hands were clammy with sweat. My heart raced with anxiety; it felt like it was going to thump its way right through my ribs and out of my chest. I had just spent my last $3,000 of savings—savings that were meant for car repairs—on some land!

I went home proudly and boasted to my wife about all the land I had bought at this auction. I remember her asking me in a frightened voice, "What do we do if you can't sell it?"

I said, "Worst-case scenario, we own land! It's not a temporary fad. It won't spoil or become obsolete. It's land, and it lasts forever. We'll be able to sell it," I assured her.

And sure enough, it did sell—even sooner than I had expected. I had bought ten parcels of land at an average price of $300 each and sold them all in thirty days at an average price of $1,200. That was a 300 percent return on my investment! Those thirty days were one of the most thrilling roller-coaster rides of my life.

Even though I had just transformed $3,000 into $12,000, my wife was terrified. She was supportive, but I got the feeling she thought that I was playing a fool's game, and we had more than a few yelling matches about it. She was scared. I was scared and we decided that I should keep pressing on and see if the process was repeatable.

Despite our combined anxiety,, I took the $9,000 profit from the first auction and went to my second auction in Arizona. This time around, I raked in more than $90,200 selling the parcels I had bought over the next six months.

Finally, our fears melted away as we realized that I had made the right decision. Even better, I knew in my heart that I would be able to buy and sell land full time and earn more money than I did at my dead-end, soul-crushing sales job.

Over the next eighteen months, I set out to master every detail of this business. I was on a mission. I wanted to look my wife in the eye with confidence and tell her I could do this full time and quit my job forever.

I worked like a man with a fire under his butt, and those eighteen months transformed my entire life forever. I felt like a hero to my wife and baby boy. I created systems and blueprints that worked with great reliability. Time and time again, I kept finding amazing land deals using my systems. And then, I figured out how to turn these deals into passive income—the holy grail of income!

Now, don't get me wrong, I made a ton of mistakes along the way. In the early days, I learned the hard way. I fell on my face more than a few times. But I just picked myself up and kept moving forward. And now, learning how to work smart has paid off big-time, because the blueprints and shortcut systems that I have put in place prevent all those costly mistakes.

It was an amazing and rewarding adventure that I'll never forget. I don't think my friend at the firm will ever realize just how much he helped me that night he shared his stories and secrets with me over a beer.

The great thing is, now I have been able to help other people the same way my buddy had helped me. I've helped people get rid of that sick feeling in their stomach that comes along with living paycheck to paycheck. I've taught people how to successfully buy and sell land and create a passive income. That's part of the meaning that financial freedom has allowed me to create in my life.

And here's the point. I'm a reasonably intelligent guy, but

honestly, I'm nothing special. The difference between me and so many other people still slaving away doing meaningless crap in cubicle hell is that right at the point when I couldn't stand it anymore, I met opportunity in the form of my friend and what he had figured out. I already had the motivation, and now I had the means.

There's no reason you can't do what I did. I can show you the means. You bring the motivation.

Oh, I forgot to mention that when I first started out in this business, my parents were mortified that I was taking on all this risk. "You quit your job, and you're working out of your house full time?" they asked with petrified looks on their faces. "How will you afford the mortgage? Or life insurance? Or baby food?" They thought I should follow conventional wisdom—get a job at a big company and retire at sixty-five. Of course, that conventional wisdom was already out of date. Defined-benefit pensions are largely a thing of the past, 401(k)s are subject to the manipulated vagaries of the stock and bond markets, and a lot of companies, if you're anywhere below C-suite, may kick you to the curb shortly before you reach retirement age and hire someone younger. But that wasn't why I kept going with my new business; it was because I was doing well in it.

When they saw how I was bringing in more and more

money each month, and how I was building up a very impressive savings account, my mom and dad wanted to learn what I was doing. I even put my parents' money into a few deals so they could share in the profits.

So part of my success was not just making money doing something I enjoyed; it was gaining the confidence of my wife and my parents and having them see the life I was creating for us. That felt even better than the money.

Now back to where it all went wrong.

In 2005, after making an average of more than $800K a year flipping raw land and working only a few hours a day, I began ramping up my material lifestyle, thinking this was the key to happiness. I bought a $1 million-plus house and even had it professionally renovated. I put my three children in expensive private schools. Eating out at restaurants, once reserved only for special occasions, became a regular weekend ritual. I remember having my parents over and bringing in a $250 steak dinner from Mastro's Steakhouse. I flew to Malibu to buy a lightly used Lexus GS430 to enjoy my first luxury car, even though I'm not a car guy and my Camry had less than 30,000 miles and was paid off. We had a nanny three days a week, we hired a housekeeper five days a week, and I was so proud to tell people that I could afford all this help for my wife whom never even asked for it. On the business side, I became complacent. Instead of looking at ways to build my business or become more efficient with systems and automation, I started a daily yoga practice, hiked for two hours a day, and brought an Xbox game console into my office to "blow off steam."

Those activities could have been beneficial in themselves—I still do them (I threw out the Xbox)—if I hadn't taken my eye off the ball and become obsessed with false symbols of success. My family, friends, and associates thought I had "made it." I looked successful, yet felt empty. It wasn't enough. And because I was turning into a hungry ghost, it could never have been enough. The sad reality was, I didn't feel like I was enough. So we began taking bigger trips during the summer. Meanwhile, business just kept humming along, as 2006 revenues exceeded 2005's. And the more I earned, the more we spent.

Parkinson's Law of Money

Basically, without my being aware of it, what I call Parkinson's law of money had taken control of my life. When we become obsessed with the pursuit of money and what it can buy, a form of Parkinson's law kicks in, even when our income rises. The original Parkinson's law states: "Work expands to fill the time allotted for its completion." Well, the law applies to money as well—something like, "Spending expands to consume available income."

Once we succumb to hungry ghost syndrome, the more money we make, the more we spend, and in the process we create our own prison of expenses and find that true financial freedom—and the meaning we can add to our lives when we attain it—keeps dancing out of reach. What should be something like heaven on earth becomes hellish, because like all unhappy souls in Buddhist tradition, we create our own hells of emptiness and our always unsatisfied desire for more. My wife and I were trapped in that emptiness. Our marriage was suffering as our self-respect began to erode. We were basically living a life of greed and gluttony, and yet neither of us had the emotional vocabulary or moral compass to get us back on track to what was truly important and what made us happy.

Thankfully (which is strange to type), the Great Recession of 2008 rolled around and forced us to examine our lives. My income began to slowly drop as the financial crisis went into full swing and we entered the Great Recession. Bit by bit, we cut back on the housekeeping and nanny. I sold my Lexus to pay taxes and leased a Prius. We had to take the kids out of private school and put them back into public school. We stopped eating out as much. Finally, in 2010, I had to short-sell the million-dollar house. We went from 4,500 square feet to a 1,700-square-foot rental. We had concealed the emptiness from ourselves with ego-feeding pride in our stuff and our lifestyle. But "Pride goes before a fall," so the cliché goes. My ego took a hard kick to the head. And when I had my panic attack, I literally took that fall headfirst.

Getting to What Matters and Being the Pebble

After that, I entered therapy and began the process of learning what was truly important to me. As we lowered our personal overhead, the business was still providing a six-figure income, and we became much happier without all the stuff and the constant expense of acquiring and maintaining all the stuff. Gradually, I stopped being a hungry ghost, and so did my wife. We started spending more time together as a family, having game nights and playing charades, going swimming and hiking, eating out a lot less, as we could no longer afford to go out every week and hire a sitter. My respect for my wife increased as she stuck by me while many of our friends were getting divorced. My children became less spoiled and enjoyed the simpler routine of our life. I began meditating and became grounded in values such as time with family, good work, and gratitude for the many blessings we were afforded.

With the knowledge we could survive anything together, my marriage became stronger. My children benefited from our relationship becoming anchored in how we aligned our values and sacrificed our egos for our family. My business began to thrive again as I innovated and created systems.

So my crash was a blessing in disguise. Today, as the economy has recovered and my income has increased dramatically from where it got to in 2008, our lifestyle remains frugal and grounded in what really makes us happy: experiences, growth, and contribution. I'll expand on this concept later. But for now, if you have ever had to sacrifice your ego and have come out of it stronger, we have that in common. If you have ever had to look your children in the eye and tell them that something they loved was no longer economically viable for your family, we have that in common, too. I look back on those experiences and can now say with certainty that what the consumer marketing world tells us will make us happy is truly a recipe for unhappiness.

However, if we can create enough passive income to exceed our fixed expenses, we free up oceans of energy to contribute in meaningful ways and fulfill our life's purpose—or at least to have enough time to explore different avenues in the pursuit of answering that higher calling. In the next chapter, I'll explain that the key is not just creating passive income but also in multiplying your sources of income. That's how I freed myself from what I call solo economic dependency.

When I was just starting out, I never dreamed I would do million-dollar land deals and flip thousands of parcels. When I started out buying and selling land, all I wanted was to be able to quit my job and make enough money to pay my bills and support my family. That's a reasonable goal, right?

But I started building momentum, and my business just kept growing and growing. In a few short years, I was able to create the ideal working situation of the three *W*s—working when I want, where I want, and with whom I want.

Here's a great example of the first *W*. Because I only work when I want, my beautiful wife, Rachel, my wonderful kids, Noah, Elan, and Ella, and I go on multiple family vacations every year. One of our favorite places to go is the Ritz-Carlton, Dove Mountain. We book an amazing suite. We go swimming, we dine on five-star meals, we go hiking, and we don't stress about the cost of the vacation. We just enjoy it!

Now, I'm not telling you this to brag. I'm telling you to make this point: no matter what we do, no matter where we go, no matter how long we stay, we don't worry about anything. And when we come home, we have more money in our bank account than we had when we left.

But a word of caution: this is true because we still have a family budget. Sure, day to day we live very comfortably, but we don't live in a huge mansion and we don't drive luxury cars that stretch our budget. My spending beyond fixed expenses is mostly on experiences—having fun with my wonderful family, traveling and seeing the world. That's one thing I learned from my time as a hungry ghost.

The other important thing I learned that I need to mention now is that to feel fulfilled, I need to give back. If I can help just one person, there's a huge ripple effect like the ripples in the surface of a pond when you drop a pebble in the water. They just keep spreading. I'm not just helping that one person; I'm helping all their relationships, so that literally everyone that person touches is affected. Think about it. If you have less financial stress, you're more relaxed and life becomes more enjoyable. Your family becomes less stressed. They all start doing better. When they do better, they start helping other people out. It's an exponential effect. So that's why I started The Land Geek and why I wrote this book. I want to be the pebble and help you become the pebble for those important to you in your life.

My goal for you is after reading this book, your mind will open to the possibilities and opportunities not just in my land investing niche but also in life. You will learn the steps I took to create passive income as well as how I did this. However, these concepts can be applied in every business. Simply put, you will learn how to buy assets pennies on the dollar. I just happen to think my raw land asset is the best and simplest to invest in. Nevertheless, even if you've never invested in real estate, my hope for you is that you will take the concepts we discuss in this book and apply them. Knowledge is power. And with power comes action. Don't stop with the knowledge. Apply it. Here we grow.

Chapter 2

The Disease of Solo Economic Dependency and How to Cure It

—

Imagine you're a dentist. You're doing well on the face of it—your practice is pretty successful. But your work is the only way you clear your monthly overhead and make a profit. You have a recurring dream that you're pulling a big wagon uphill. Sitting in that wagon are your dental technician, your office assistant, the hygienist who comes in three days a week, your accountant, your insurance agents, your landlord, your dental suppliers, and the dental equipment reps. And if you unhitch yourself from that heavy wagon, you know it's going to start rolling downhill, faster and faster. You wake from that dream in a cold sweat.

And you know what? Your attorney may be having the same bad dream, only with the legal profession's equivalents sitting in her wagon. But her problem is basically just the same as yours.

Now imagine you're a bit lower down on the professional food chain—a freelance graphic designer and web developer. You aren't paying any staff, but you have office rent and bills to pay, especially your phone and internet service—you need premium bandwidth and connection speeds for all those big files—not to mention software upgrades, software as a service (SaaS) subscriptions, and cloud storage. And you're constantly threatened by "mushroom" companies—the kind that have an office or two poking up in the United States but whose real staffs of dozens of designers and developers are hidden away in Bangalore or Bulgaria, earning pennies on every dollar you charge so that their firms can always underbid you. That means you're working harder and harder and retraining yourself constantly as you search for niches where there's still a decent hourly rate for your services.

Finally, imagine you're me as I was shortly before I became the Land Geek. As I talked about in the previous chapter, I was an investment banker doing cold calling, a miserable job working for a horrible boss, with a wife and new baby at home—and barely scraping by from month to month. Like so many working people in the United States today, I was in a Red Queen's race.

The Red Queen's Race

The Red Queen's race happens in Lewis Carroll's *Through the Looking-Glass* when the Red Queen and Alice are running without stopping but also without moving forward.

"Well, in our country," said Alice, still panting a little, "you'd generally get to somewhere else—if you run very fast for a long time, as we've been doing."

"A slow sort of country!" said the Queen. "Now, here, you see, it takes all the running you can do, to keep in the same place. If you want to get somewhere else, you must run at least twice as fast as that!"

In fact, most Americans are now running as fast as they can, working as many hours as they can—and not even staying in the same place but slowly slipping backward. That's why so many couples fight about things, such as the price of healthy baby food, that they shouldn't ever have to fight about. That's why in most families in America today, both wife and husband are working outside the home, sometimes as many as three jobs between them. And according to a recent study, most don't even have $1,000 in their checking and savings accounts combined.

That's the Red Queen's race, and more and more people are losing that race or barely holding their own. The days when you could go to work for a company in your twenties and count on a job for life are gone. Often, if you did a reasonably good job, advance within the company ranks, you'd have a defined-benefit pension waiting for you at sixty-five; that's long gone. In the vast majority of cases, job security is a thing of the past, as is income security.

Solo Economic Dependency: The Trap

To understand how I came to view the implications of all this, let's flash back to the first job I got straight out of college, when I was twenty-three years old. I was a dental business broker. Most of my days consisted of two activities: I helped dentists grow their practices through mergers, and I helped retiring dentists sell their practices. At twenty-three, seriously wet behind the ears, I had no real idea what I was doing when I started. However, I was lucky enough to acquire a mentor at the company named Raj, who had both an MBA and a degree in chemical engineering. Raj taught me how to create pro formas—the financial statements and projections prepared by the seller of a business to show prospective buyers—how to recast earnings, and how to appraise dental practices. However, that was just the nuts and bolts of dental brokering.

What I really learned there was that dentists, doctors, chiropractors, and most other people in the business world were afflicted with a disease that I call solo economic dependency. From our perspective as brokers who saw the balance sheets, it looked as if the dentist was working for his staff and suppliers and not the other way around. That's because if he didn't have his hands in a patient's mouth, he wasn't making any money.

Since then, I've come to understand that the same condition afflicts the great majority. If you have a regular job, think about how much time each month you spend on that job working for your landlord or your mortgage lender, how much time you spend working for whoever owns the note on your car, how much of it you spend working for your phone company and your ISP, and so on. A lot, right? So no wonder that when you have solo economic dependency, there's a good chance you'll end up as another contestant in the Red Queen's race, going nowhere fast and getting older day by day as your life is used up in the endless struggle. Ouch.

The Dream of the Perfect Business

Thinking about the situation our dentist clients were in, Raj and I would dream and debate about the perfect business. We concluded that the perfect business would have a few essential characteristics:

1. No physical inventory
2. A one-time sale and then recurring revenue
3. Built-in pain or hassle for the customer to opt out of that service or product

4. A niche without competitive pricing pressures

Can you guess what we first decided would be the perfect business based on these criteria? Wait for it...selling life insurance. It certainly met the first three criteria. Unfortunately, life insurance presented some major problems.

To begin with, selling life insurance is highly competitive. Second, it's not much fun to actually sell; most people avoid their life insurance agents like the plague, and you have to keep prodding them with emails and other communications to get them to pay attention to their policies. Third, there are pricing pressures, as life insurance is a commodity. Not so perfect.

Software companies such as Microsoft, which in those days ruled the personal computer software market almost unchallenged through Windows and Office—or Oracle, which similarly dominated the database market—looked as though they might be the perfect business at that time. After all, they met all four criteria by the early 1990s. No physical inventory, one-time sale and recurring revenue, huge pain and hassle to opt out, and little or no competitive pressure. Think "installed base." That installed base—software installed on countless millions of computers in offices around the world, which transitioning away from in even a medium-sized business is hugely costly and time-consuming—is the most important reason

Oracle and Microsoft are still multibillion-dollar companies. But even before Apple's rise to market prominence after the return of Steve Jobs to the company, we could see the continual pressure to constantly innovate within the Microsoft model. And as we've seen from Microsoft's subsequent history, under innovation pressure, even a giant can stumble.

Well, after working with Raj, I got a job at an investment banking firm that specialized in mergers and acquisitions with private equity groups buying up medium-sized companies in leveraged buyouts. During my five years of working in that industry, I probably looked at more than a thousand companies. And after speaking with hundreds of CEOs and CFOs, often of really interesting companies doing really ingenious things with really creative business models, always in the back of my mind I could hear Raj's voice whispering to me, "Is this the perfect business?" The answer, on reflection, was always no.

Saying Good-Bye to the Red Queen: Steps to the Perfect Business

In the last chapter, I told you how things were for me and my family right before, by a stroke of amazing luck, I met my friend and took action on the land business. I started buying and selling raw land on a booming web platform called eBay, and my average profit was 300 percent. That's why I was scribbling frantically on bar napkins.

Buying and selling raw land all by itself looked like the perfect business—almost:

- Unlike almost anything else you can buy, raw land lasts forever.
- Not only that, but raw land can easily be improved to increase its value.
- Yet unlike a commercial building or a private home—or anything else you might put there to improve it—raw land has a low cost of ownership.
- And even undeveloped, every piece of land is unique, and even though it is a commodity, it has tremendous pricing flexibility.

The best part about raw land, as you recall I told my wife when I got into the business, was that even if I couldn't sell my land, at least we owned it! Our land was an asset that cost very little to own, that would increase in value, and that we actually had control over. We couldn't eat money, I told her, but if we had to, we could cultivate our land and live off it. So land was the ultimate asset to own.

It's easy to see how buying and selling raw land met Raj's and my perfect business criteria 1 and 4: no physical inventory (the land itself doesn't count, because it just sits there) and little in the way of competitive pricing pressure, because every piece of land is unique. Criterion 3 doesn't really count in a simple land sale: once the buyer signs the deed, the land belongs to the buyer and you, the seller, have the cash. Plus, you don't have to worry about maintaining or protecting the land.

But what about criterion 3—a one-time sale and then recurring revenue? That was the missing piece in my friend's business model, which made it less than perfect. There was no ongoing relationship with the customer—the buyer—and no recurring revenue. The answer, I discovered, was owner financing. I'll be talking a lot more about this in later chapters, but here's the basic idea. You buy a property for $0.20 to $0.30 on the dollar, and then you sell it for full market value or a slight market discount on a note with interest. In many cases, you get your initial investment back from just the down payment when you sell it on easy financing terms like an easy automobile payment. Think about it. A lot of prospective customers might not be able to afford paying thousands of dollars in cash, but they can afford to make easy payments of $299 or so a month. So when you start selling the land you've bought with owner financing, you have not only got your recurring revenue, but you've also just tremendously expanded your customer base. And the more owners you have making those monthly payments, the less solo your income will be.

Say you have ten customers paying installments on notes you hold from them for land they bought from you. If one of them defaults and you end up repossessing the land, you still have the other nine—and you can turn around and resell that one parcel (and get another down payment at a lower cost basis). What's more, you have met criterion 3 as well, because the consequence of defaulting on those monthly payments is going to be a huge painful hassle for your customer. That's a big incentive for them to keep those checks coming. Now—in a somewhat different way than Raj and I imagined—you have met all four of our essential criteria for the perfect business.

However, to make the business even better, you don't want it to consume your life. We've all seen the tales of entrepreneurs who sacrifice years of their lives and often their close personal and familial relationships outside of work—to building their companies and then to keeping them growing. Yes, you will have to put in some long hours of hard work to get your land business off the ground, but it doesn't have to keep going that way—which after all is the point. Remember the Mexican fisherman and the Harvard MBA? Here is an introduction to things I learned to do for you to have a life while still running a highly successful operation.

Working Smart versus Working Hard

With today's technology, entrepreneurs are able to get more done in less time than ever before. As we transition from an industrial economy to a connection economy, understanding this leverage becomes critical. I like technology—I'm a geek, after all—but I do not spend my days converting videos, posting to forums and blogs, producing my own topography maps of land, or even sending out my own land offers. All I do is create a process, document it for an outsourced virtual assistant to execute at a fraction of the cost, and spend an hour or so a day making sure it was done right. That way, I'm focused on working *on* my business and not *in* my business. I'll discuss in detail how I do this in a later chapter. For now, I want to talk a bit more about what it will take for you to get there in terms of attitude, mental preparation, and strategy.

However, before we get into that, we need to address one more question I've often been asked:

"Mark, why not just make as much money as possible and invest in the stock market and retire at sixty-five?"

First of all, if that's the track you are currently on, how's it going? If I had to bet, I'd predict it's not going that well and that you're probably stressed out and wondering if you'll ever be able to retire. Because everyone's needs and spending habits are different, here is a link to a page where you can calculate how much you would need to save to retire. When I went there, I plugged in that I would simply need a fairly modest retirement income of $150,000 a year to live the lifestyle I would want in order to eat well, travel, pay medical expenses, take the grandkids on vacations, and so on.

I discovered that I would need to save $4,228,960 if I wanted to live to age ninety with an average yield on my investments of 6 percent.

Retirement Estimations

Inputs

Required Income (Current Dollars)	$ 150000
Required Income (Future Dollars)	$ 233695.11
Number of Years Until Retiring	15
Number of Years After Retiring	25
Annual Inflation (on Required Income)	3 %
Annual Yield on Balance	6.0 %

4,228,960 Dollars!!! Yikes!
You will need $ 4228960.47

http://www.banksite.com/calc/retire

However, it took me only three years to accumulate enough land notes to exceed this income on a passive basis. Plus, unlike the stock market, I have total control over the land. I create the pricing, choose the location, decide if and what type of improvements I can make, and where and how I want to market my property. As a result, I have essentially created an income stream for myself backed by an asset, and I can duplicate the process again and again. However, if you invest your money in the stock and bond markets, how much control do you really have? Do you completely understand the business? Are you 100 percent confident that management is working for the shareholders and not themselves? If you're on this track and things are going well, then great! However, if the prospect of saving more than $4 million seems impossible to you, then continue reading.

How I Define Passive versus Active Income

Let's be completely honest. Acquiring land, then marketing the land, and finally managing the notes doesn't sound like passive income to you, does it? Well, I could argue that if we define passive income as having to do absolutely nothing, then there is no such thing as passive income. You still had to earn the money to put into the bank to earn a passive income on the interest. That earning was work. So let's be clear—when you first start out, there will be some serious work involved. However, in this book I will teach you how to outsource most of the work of the business so that you don't have to manage the notes, market the property, or even send out the letters or go to the auctions yourself to buy the parcels. However, you will have to manage your team and make sure that they're doing things correctly. Don't worry about that either. I will teach you how to put systems in place so that the process is clear and straightforward. This, in turn, helps your team to become effective and accomplish your goals.

I define passive income as making money in your sleep after you've set up your systems and you're no longer doing all or most of the work to earn that income.

Being Realistic: Step by Step Away from Solo Economic Dependency

"The tragedy of life doesn't lie in not reaching your goal. The tragedy lies in having no goal to reach.

—BENJAMIN MAYS

When you first start putting my systems into action and start making money, please don't quit your day job. As with any new endeavor, you will have your struggles as you get your arms around the nuances of this business. Only pursue buying and selling land full time once your income exceeds your full-time job or you have enough savings to handle the inevitable business dip. That's what I did. That's what many of my clients have done. I kept working for eighteen long months at my horrible investment banking job while working my land business part time. Only after my land income exceeded my income at my full-time job did I take the plunge.

If you've come to the point where you're no longer interested in passively watching your life unfold one day at a time—even while you're running as fast as you can in the Red Queen's race—but instead want to actively and deliberately begin forming a plan to step off Her Majesty's invisible treadmill, now is the time to start setting goals. The problem for most people is that they don't take a systematic approach to setting up their goals. Below is my goal-setting system to get you started:

The SMART Goal System

Specific
Measurable
Achievable
Relevant
Time bound

If you're creating goals that meet these criteria, you become much more focused. The method will also let you keep score—M for measurable and T for time bound—to know if and when you need to adapt your approach to achieve your goals.

As Peter Drucker is famous for saying, "Whatever is measured is managed." The same is true of setting goals. One of my favorite books is *The 12 Week Year* by Brian P. Moran and Michael Lennington. The argument made is that most companies set annual goals, then Parkinson's law sets in and they don't really focus hard until the end of the year. With the twelve-week year you focus every day on your twelve-week goal.

The goal has to be specific. No vague pie-in-the-sky types of goals such as "I want to be wealthy." The goal of "I want to close twelve deals in twelve weeks" is specific. It's also measurable; there is no ambiguity about what needs to be done each day to measure that goal. It's achievable; clearly, a deal a week in our business isn't unrealistic. Plus, it's relevant; this is the business we have chosen and it stays within our focus and expertise. Finally, it's a time bound goal: twelve weeks to close twelve deals. It's very simple, yet a very powerful and impactful approach to goal setting. Without setting goals, it's like you're trying to hit a moving target and your brain won't be hardwired to hitting that goal.

Try the SMART system and then join the Land Geek Motivation and Wealth Creation Group on Facebook and tell us your results.

Scott Todd, one of our star students and Land Geek–certified coaches, and the cohost of my podcast, *The Art of Passive Income*, set a goal to close three hundred deals his second year in the business. Instead, he closed 198. He did more than $1 million in revenue but didn't achieve his goal. Nevertheless, he was ecstatic as he worked his twelve-week year system because the year before, he closed sixty-eight deals. He set an ambitious goal using a 10X-type mindset to motivate himself and knowing full well that if he did 150 deals, he would have been happy.

This is the power of big goals and priming your brain to achieve whatever you want to achieve in life. You just have to believe it's realistic so you work with a focused intensity that moves effortlessly through any obstacle in your way.

In the next chapter, let's explore why we should invest in land and not other assets.

Chapter 3

Why Land Is a
Unique Asset (and
the Ideal Business)

Real estate is an imperishable asset, ever increasing in value.
It is the most solid security that human ingenuity has devised.
It is the basis of all security and about the only indestructi-
ble security.

—RUSSELL SAGE, AMERICAN
FINANCIER AND POLITICIAN

When you hear the name Jeff Bezos, you think of Amazon, the biggest online retailer, right? But Bezos is also a huge landowner. So are Ted Turner and Warren Buffett. And why do you think many of the savviest and most successful businesspeople in the world are pouring millions, if not billions, into land?

Why in the world did I pick land? Why in the world should you pick land? What's so great about land?

Well, land is simple. It's simple because you don't have to deal with the risks and headaches that you would typically run into with developed real estate or other kinds of property, let alone with investing in the stock or currency markets.

Let me break that down a bit.

First of all, like the Dude in *The Great Lebowski*, land abides. It's just there. It was there long before human beings walked the earth, and unless we get a lot more careful soon with the whole natural environment that sustains us, it'll be there after human beings are gone. I can pass the land in my family trust down to my children and they can pass it down to theirs, but even "unto the seventh generation" is less than the blink of an eye on the scale of the history of the earth.

That doesn't mean there's never any change on the land. An old friend of mine, an artist and retired teacher, owns a four-acre property in rural Lake County, California. She had a modest house, a guest cottage, and some other outbuildings on her land, as well as a vegetable garden and some pretty trees. In 2015, a huge wildfire swept through the county. Luckily, she and her family were down staying in their other home in San Francisco at the time, so they were unharmed. However, the fire completely destroyed every building and tree on her property. All that was left, literally, was ashes and charred stumps. That said, she still has the land, and if she can hold on to it long enough, its value will rise back up along with the grass and the trees.

To underline the point: nobody can actually steal or destroy your land, even if what's on it can be destroyed. I mean, someone could load up a wheelbarrow full of soil or rocks from your land and run off like a bandit, but guess what? There's more underneath. Your land will always be there.

Along with that, there's virtually no maintenance. I personally own more than eighty properties in my family trust. Not one of these properties costs me anything to take care of, and not one requires any effort from me in terms of maintenance, which is great, because these properties are directly in the path of growth and I have no intention of ever selling them.

Number two, you won't be troubled by the four Rs of developed real estate—renters, rehabs, renovations, and rodents. According to almost everyone, the biggest appeal of real estate investing is the rental income and capital appreciation on the houses, apartment buildings, or commercial buildings. Well, my neighbor, an anesthesiologist who is a buddy of mine, owns twenty-two rental properties. He has constant tenant issues and maintenance headaches, and he has to save a significant amount of money every month for upkeep. We both do very well financially with our investments, but my weekends and his weekends are vastly different. While I'm watching basketball, snacking on carrots and hummus, and enjoying a couple of cold beers, he is busy taking care of tenant issues all weekend.

Back in the day when I first started buying land, I followed the wisdom of the herd and tried a fix-and-flip here in Carefree, Arizona, with a buddy of mine. Well, I'm not what you would consider a very handy guy. In fact, my wife has our handyman, Darin, on emergency speed dial.

After three months of laboring on the house, depending on subcontractors to do the work we weren't qualified to do, paying the Realtor's commission, and factoring in our time, we made money on paper, but in no way was it even remotely worth the effort we put into it. We were both exhausted and miserable. We sold the property, and I went back to raw land.

Number three, unlike stocks and bonds, you have total control over the asset. You can pick the location, you can improve the land, you can use it for something productive, and you can even live on it if you want to. Most people, though, follow the herd and invest in the stock market. But the stock market is really just a huge casino, and the game is rigged—legally, for the most part, but still rigged. (You only have to look at the revolving door between the Securities and Exchange Commission, which is supposed to regulate the equities markets, and the big investment banks and hedge funds to see why it's legal. And let's not even get into all the former senators and congress-men awarded lucrative seats on the boards of those huge firms.) The investment banks and hedge funds, with their thousands of shares in hundreds of traded companies, largely control how any given stock moves, even if news of the company's earnings projections does still play a role.

The only really sound strategy for investing in the stock market is Warren Buffett's: buy blue-chip stocks—shares in very well-established and stable companies whose value is never going to dip very far for very long—and hold on to them for decades. Of course, the only problem with that strategy is that those shares are very expensive, so you have to have a lot of cash available to buy them in the first place. The brokers and "advisers" want you to invest your hard-earned money where they have the most control. Would you rather control your wealth or blindly hand over your dollars to someone who doesn't care about your best interests?

Some other people try their hand at currency trading in

what's called forex—short for foreign exchange. Essentially, you're betting on the relative values of currencies rising or falling, which they do constantly. The problem here is that much of the money in forex trading—like much of the money in the stock market—is made by what's called high-speed algorithmic microtrading. In case you haven't heard of this, it means using very sophisticated software applications to buy and sell on tiny price movements—think six places past the decimal point—shifts in the values of currencies in equally tiny fractions of a second. Unless you either pay a company that does this to trade for you or you're a genius software developer and write one of your own, you're going to be locked out of the most lucrative side of currency trading. And guess what? That's how a lot of trading on the stock market is done now, too—by the big institutional investors. They have no interest in letting you in (read *Flash Boys* by Michael Lewis for more information).

With land, on the other hand, you control the asset. And in addition to control, land gives you the opportunity to produce income. Also, the market value of your land can increase dramatically with population growth. As we approach ten billion people on Earth, usable raw land is just going to become scarcer and scarcer.

Imagine buying land ten years ago in North Dakota before the shale oil fields were discovered. Or what if you had owned land in New York City or Los Angeles thirty years ago when these cities were experiencing huge growth? I guarantee, if you think about it, you know someone (or someone who knows someone) who bought a piece of raw land in the path of growth, and they became an instant millionaire.

Number four—this is a big one—land actually can provide cash flow. Yep, just raw, unimproved land. You can structure your sales so that you get cash flow for years and years and years. And that's a big part of what we're going to talk about later in this book.

Number five, there is virtually no competition in the land business. How many people do you know who talk about land investing? Most people think that land is super expensive. They say land is something that costs millions of dollars and that it's only for the rich. Or they say land is for developers who love to take big risks.

You know what? That's probably true for downtown Phoenix, Los Angeles, New York City, Atlanta, and Boston where quarter-acre lots sell for $3 million, right?

The good news is, we are not focusing on these $3 million lots. Not even close! We're going to look for lots or acreage that cost less than $30,000. We want property in the outskirts of big cities, in smaller towns, and in rural areas—areas that nobody actually looks at, talks about, or analyzes.

And here's the open secret. Even though most investors overlook the land that we're going to seek out, there is a huge demand for these properties, especially right now. A recent study found that 9 percent of Americans—fewer than one in ten—would choose to live in a major city today. Twenty-four percent of all Americans want to live in a small town away from big cities, and 22 percent want to live specifically in a rural area. The primary reasons given? Cities are full of crime, traffic, congestion, and crowds. Hopefully, we can agree that this market is massive.

The Ideal Business

In this book, I'm not only going to discuss how flipping land will increase your wealth, but I'm also going to talk about how you can leverage your land to create passive income. It's like rental income without tenants, so it's way better than rental income. As I explained earlier, no four Rs, no maintenance.

Once you get started in this business, you'll eventually start finding properties that you really like. In fact, you'll like them so much that you'll want to keep them, which is great. You don't have to sell every property you buy.

You'll be wise to hold on to properties that you know are in the path of growth.

For example, I bought land in a subdivision outside of Albuquerque that is ripe for development. I'm just going to hold on to that land for my family and me. Maybe I'll build a house on it someday, or maybe I'll sell it for a massive gain.

But, what makes it even better is this: no matter what your current financial situation is, no matter where you live, no matter how little spare time you have, the land business will make an incredible difference in your life if you apply the systems I teach. Even if you've never bought a scrap of land in your life, you will be up and running in a few short weeks. Even if you have more than fifty years of experience in real estate, you will find my systems to be completely game changing.

And if you have only a few hundred dollars to get started investing in land, it's no problem at all. You can take $100 and make it $400. Then you can go from $400 to $1,600, $1,600 to $6,400, $6,400 to $25,600, $25,600 to $102,400, $102,400 to $409,600, $409,600 to $1,638,400. You don't need a lot of money to get started in this business. You just need to take action.

When I started investing in land, remember, I was dead

broke, squabbling with my wife about the price of organic baby food. And only three years later, I had built up enough passive income to exceed $150,000 per year and a 6 percent return. That's real wealth. Can you see how making more than $150K in your sleep could have a dramatic effect on your life and your retirement?

Yet the land business required no travel, no maintenance, very little up-front money, and virtually no competition. So here's my first deal in New Mexico. I bought a half-acre parcel for $300 and flipped it online for $1,200. Now for the very first deal that I did, I made 300 percent in one week. Common sense was screaming from the rooftops, "Just keep doing that, Mark."

The second deal that I did was an inexpensive subdivision in southern Arizona I bought from a tax sale. Now, this is going to blow your mind: there was almost no one at this auction, just a few locals and me. And the locals seemed to have no interest at all in this property. The starting bid was $50. No one was bidding, so I asked the auctioneer if she would lower it. She said, "Sure, $25." Still no bids. I said I'd bid $1. I got bid up to $3! I ended up buying hundreds of lots that day for what I would pay for dinner at a nice restaurant. Then I sold all those parcels for more than 3,000 percent profit—or more than $90K in just six months. Not one customer complaint and not one refund. And get this: I had never seen the properties in person, only on my computer.

Here's another deal I did my first year sending out offers. I bought a five-acre parcel in Colorado for $500. I sold it a week later for $4,000 on Craigslist. That's seven times my money.

How about another deal? I bought nine half-acre lots in Florida near Fort Myers with utilities and paved roads in a subdivision for only $250 each. I sold them all on easy financing terms for $10K down plus a monthly payment of more than $900 for fifteen years at 9 percent interest.

I did a deal with a student of mine, Tory, who found thirty 40-acre parcels owned by one distressed seller. We bought all 1,200 acres for less than $60 an acre. Tory sold his fifteen parcels on terms at $500 an acre. He's going to make more than $300,000 just on one deal! This is the power of the land business. It can literally change your life overnight.

As I've mentioned, we're focusing on buying properties less than $30,000. And selling them is ridiculously easy today with all the internet platforms available. Without the internet, we'd be like the old-time land sellers buying radio spots and putting up billboards. Today, in less time than it takes to shave, you can market and sell a property online.

I want to stress the point of easy to implement. Now, easy

does NOT mean without effort. It just means that I've removed all of the brain damage involved with figuring out how to bring in your target market and how to get more buyers than you can handle.

Secret Advertisers of Land for Sale

I've talked a lot about the benefits and advantages of investing in land. Let's get into how it actually works. You may be very surprised, because the concept is deceptively simple. It all starts with this one simple fact: all over the country, there are people who don't want their property anymore. How do I know this? Well, they're secretly advertising it. Let me explain.

These landowners haven't paid their property taxes. And when we don't value something, we don't pay for it, right? Or we may be in some type of financial or personal distress. Many of these landowners just want to get rid of their property. And your jaw will hit the floor and bounce when you discover how many of these owners will sell you their property for next to nothing. Sometimes they'll even give it to you for free just to get rid of their tax burden.

It's hard to wrap your head around this until you see it firsthand. Every month, when you do this business consistently, you're going to get properties for pennies on the dollar or even for free.

Why don't these people want to keep their property and why don't they value it? Well, owners want to get rid of their land for quite a variety of reasons. They might have lost their job. They might be going through a divorce. They might have inherited their land from a relative who passed away, and they have no clue what to do with it. There are boatloads of reasons, more than I need to detail at this point. So what happens when landowners don't want their properties? They stop paying their property taxes and start going down the road to tax foreclosure.

Tax Lien Auctions: Not What I'm Talking About, and Why Not

Let's be crystal clear. This is NOT a tax lien investment strategy I'm talking about. My model has nothing to do with the tax lien system. What's a tax lien auction, you may be asking? The process varies by state, but here's how it generally works. When property owners don't pay their property taxes, tax collectors wait the period required by state law and then put those unpaid property taxes up for auction—the tax liability on the property, not the property itself. At auction, that liability becomes a tax lien, a claim on the property.

In most states, the bidder willing to pay the most cash for the tax lien wins the auction. Some states, though, have a bid-down process, where investors' bids indicate how much interest they're willing to accept on their investment, and the lowest bidder wins. But in all cases, the tax collector takes the payment for the overdue taxes from the winning bid, let's say yours. In exchange for your cash, you acquire a lien on the property. So as the winning bidder, you can get a return on your investment in one of two ways: interest on your bid amount or ownership of the property. If the owner redeems their property by paying the overdue taxes within the time allowed under state law, you get your investment capital back, plus the amount of interest allowed in your state—usually set by statute and ranging from 10 to as high as 18 percent, with the average around 12 percent. So it is a good way to make a passive return of say 12–18 percent. However, would you rather make 12–18 percent or 300–5,000 percent? I think I know the answer.

But what if what you're really after is the actual property? Well, about 98 percent of delinquent owners redeem their property within a year. If the owner fails to redeem, though, you don't just get it as if you bought it. You have to file a lawsuit seeking title to it. That process can be complicated, costly, and time-consuming. And that's on top of the redemption period, which can be years. In Arizona, for example, you have to wait three years to foreclose on the lien. In some states, it may be only a year or two. Still, we're talking years, not days.

All of the above is why I don't recommend the tax lien method.

Tax Deed Auctions: Not Best for Beginners (Even Though That's How I Began)

Buying properties at tax deed auctions is something I teach as another method of acquisition, but that's not what I want you to focus on at first.

That's because auctions can be competitive, depending on the market you're in. At some auctions, egos get out of control and the bidding goes so high that properties end up selling for retail. When auctions get competitive like that, they become a huge waste of your time, and that's definitely not what we want.

Here's a real-life example. Not long ago, I went to an auction in northern Nevada. Almost two hundred people showed up. The room was packed and people were ready to scrap with one another over the 150 properties up for auction. Now, if you have two hundred people bidding on 150 properties, what happens? Exactly—the price goes up.

One of the golden rules I stress is, never, ever overpay. You don't want to buy properties at auction that sell for 80–90 percent of market value or higher.

Wait a minute, Mark, you may be thinking. You just told me that you started out by going to tax deed auctions, and now you're telling me not to bother with them?

Uhmm, not exactly. If you can find a tax deed auction that has low competition (which I'll explain later how to find), then by all means start buying those properties for pennies on the dollar like I did when I was starting out.

But there's a better way I learned later on: avoid that competition altogether by snapping up properties before they hit the tax lien or deed auction. And that's what I'm going to tell you about next. I teach you to avoid competition and to avoid the expensive and time-consuming state foreclosure process. You do it by writing offer letters to the vacant land owners.

Now, I know there are some systems out there that teach similar letter-writing campaigns to find properties. The thing is, with these systems, a lot of the time you unwittingly get into the land appraisal business. If you encourage your potential sellers to call you, for example, you'll get a lot of tire kickers wasting your time because they're curious about what their land is worth.

My offer system is completely unique in that we don't ever have to talk with the sellers. We avoid all the long, drawn-out conversations about what they think the property is worth and what you think the property is worth. We get straight to the point and right down to business.

Now, I understand why these other systems encourage

you to talk with potential sellers. You end up generating more responses overall, and then the gurus who taught you this can brag about the high response rates.

But I don't care about response rates. Response rates are meaningless if you don't close deals. I care about the closing rate on deals. For example, I sent out one hundred letters recently in Colorado. I received back seven signed purchase agreements. That's a 7 percent response ratio.

How would you like to know that every time you sent out one hundred offers that you would buy three to seven properties and make more than 300 to 1000 percent on each property? That's how you are ultimately going to build your real estate portfolio and empire. You are going to make offers on a very consistent basis and eventually build a system that removes you from the equation so you can focus on the most important aspects of your business. We'll talk more about that later.

This is NOT a small little niche market. I can say from experience that the market is actually massive because since 2001, my deal flow has never stopped. Just look at the number of people who owe back taxes in this country on raw land.

There's a website I discovered called TaxSaleLists.com, where they keep track of all the properties out there on which the owners are not paying their taxes. You can see that comes out to about 23,962,000 properties whose owners are behind. And not paying taxes on a property is almost the same as putting up a big flashing sign that says, "Please Buy My Land! I Don't Want It Any More!"

So let me ask you, now do you think this is a big market? Of course, it's a huge market. And if we look at the numbers, we know that at one time most of these same people—the ones who didn't just inherit their land—were buying property themselves. That's a healthy market. It has the flexibility to grow or contract without having major effects on the overall economics of this business. Now, not every one of these twenty-three million people are going to want to sell their property to you for pennies on the dollar. Some of them have simply forgotten to pay their taxes. Some probably just pay their property taxes every two years. There are many reasons, so we can't assume everyone wants to sell.

Nevertheless, if just a tiny fraction of those twenty-three million people do want to sell, we have a ridiculously large market to enter. Plus, it's not like housing, where you are competing against multibillion-dollar private equity groups and hedge funds. Housing is easier to understand than land, but land is so much better. I bet if you go to a REIA (Real Estate Investor Association) meeting and there are 100 people in the room, 99 of them will be house flippers, house wholesalers or landlords. You and I would be the only land investors there. That illustrates just how little competition there is in our huge niche.

We are going to discuss in detail how you can make MORE money from buying and selling raw land than you can from flipping houses. And you're going to learn how you can make MORE money selling land with owner financing than you can from owning rental houses. Even better, I'll show you how you can do this without the headaches that come along with flipping houses or being a landlord. Are you ready to go on this journey with me?

Chapter 4

How to Print Your Own Money (Legally!)

———

Let's jump into the details of how this system works by talking about the five key steps of creating serious wealth with land investing.

Step 1: Find the sellers who no longer want their property.

Step 2: Send out "top dollar" (25-30 cents on the dollar) offers to the people we find in Step 1.

Step 3: Analyze the deal (due diligence).

Step 4: Market the property on internet platforms that already have a lot of traffic.

Step 5: Sell the property.

Now, you just went from having zero land selling experience to closing your first deal in only five steps. And then—the best part—you take your profits and reinvest into more land. Rinse and repeat.

Step 1: Find the Sellers Who No Longer Want Their Property

Like we discussed earlier, what you're looking for is people who are advertising to the world that they don't want their land anymore.

As a first action step, contact the local county assessor or treasurer. Then take that list of people and filter it down by criteria such as the price range, where the owner lives, and how long they have owned the property.

There are a whole lot more criteria that we need to look at, but we'll get to that at the end, as I don't want you to drink from a firehose in this book. Essentially, the result we get from filtering this list is this: a really good percentage of the people receiving your offers will happily sell you their land for pennies on the dollar.

Here's a recent case study. One of my students, Jeff Akstin, executed our letter writing campaign so well that he was able to buy thirty 5-acre parcels in Colorado from a distressed seller at an average price of $222, plus a few thousand dollars in back taxes. His total cash profit from this deal was more than $30,000 in two months. Plus, he sold some of the parcels on easy seller-financing terms, and he is now getting an extra $1,000 a month in passive income.

Keep in mind, we're not talking about junk lots. We're talking about quality lots that have views, good access, and nearby amenities. And get this: if Jeff had found this deal and didn't have the money to buy the thirty parcels himself, he could have easily wholesaled out these properties without putting any money down. Wholesaling is another strategy I teach with lease options, but I don't want to get ahead of myself.

For Jeff, making an extra $30K in two months made a significant impact in his life. But most importantly, his time investment on this deal was minimal.

Step 2: Send Out Lowball Offers to the Potential Sellers We Found in Step 1

Now, my offers are unique. I have tested every aspect of all my letters that I send out. The typical direct response rate for direct marketing is something like 0.5 percent response. Think of your own mailbox where you get auto loan offers, magazine offers, and so forth. Very few people actually respond. A half percent is all the marketer needs to make money on the promotion.

Now in real estate, some people use yellow letters that look like handwritten letters, and they're getting a 2–3 percent response rate. If you're in a short-sell area, you might get like a 1 or 2 percent response rate.

The response rate my students and I get is between 3–5 percent. Do you think it would be great to get three to five amazing deals for every hundred letters you sent out?

Here's the thing: because my letters and postcards are so well-tested and because these landowners don't actually get much mail, they are much more receptive. Plus, you can't find these deals in the multiple listing service (MLS) because the property owners haven't even listed their land with a Realtor.

My letters are one page and don't offer up any room for negotiations. Again, we don't want to waste time being in the appraisal business. We want legitimate motivated sellers, people who are super interested in selling because they don't want their property anymore.

As a result, every time you run one of my mailing campaigns, it's like collecting checks at the post office every day. The best part is, people save the letters and send them in months later. Plus, we all know in real estate, we make our money on the buy and not on the sell. These accepted offers are just that, money in your bank.

Put another way, how would you like to spend $20 on a mailing and make $3,000? You can't get that type of return in the stock market.

Step 3: Analyze the Deal (Due Diligence)

What you want to do when analyzing these properties is check a few simple things. You or your virtual assistant can jump on a computer and do a five- to ten-minute property value check online. If you don't want to train your own virtual assistant how to conduct proper due diligence we have our own trained team in the Philippines that can assist. Learn more at www.vas.thelandgeek.com.

Due diligence may sound intimidating, but here's the rub: because you can leverage the power of the internet, because there are aerial pictures of just about every piece of land on Earth, all you need to do is get a ballpark value of that property.

You don't even have to be physically at the property. As a matter of fact, I can't tell you the last time, in the thousands of deals I've done, that I've actually set foot on the property. Plus, with the inexpensive crowdsourcing available online, you can easily hire a local to take pictures and videos of the land for you and prepare an entire property report for almost nothing.

Buying sight unseen may sound crazy at first, but with the technology and crowdsourcing you can leverage online, you don't have to stress about not being at the property.

Plus, I don't actually do the work. I outsource all the due diligence to my virtual assistants who creates all of the maps I need for about $3-$5 an hour.

More importantly, you can literally do this business from anywhere. All you need is an inexpensive computer or just access to someone else's computer, even if it's just one at your local library. The only tools your really need are access to a computer, access to the internet, and a telephone. It doesn't get much simpler.

Being from Arizona, my family and I love to get away from the heat sometimes. One year, we took six weeks and went to Lake Tahoe. I just brought my laptop and was in business. It doesn't matter where you are in the world, as long as you have access to a computer and the internet, you can do this business.

As a matter of fact, I have several international students from the Netherlands, Australia, and Belgium who are working this model to improve their lives and make additional passive income for their families.

Clients of mine, Sean Rickman and Rachael Mueller created

enough passive income to quit their software engineering and sales jobs. They then began traveling Europe together with just a laptop, a virtual mailbox service and a few virtual assistants to close deals while exploring the world.

Here's a testimonial from Jeff Akstin that I want to share:

Hey, Mark,

I just want to say thank you for taking my business to the next level.

I started with your investor's toolkit, and with your guidance, I went from a land business making only 5–10K a year to 50K this year, and it's only October!

This week has been great! I sold two parcels of land that I have owned for about a month for 17K profit, and I just purchased fourteen lots for $877 each and they will sell for $6,000 each on terms! These deals happen for me weekly.

Thanks for your help, and I look forward to working with you in the future.

Jeff Akstin

Now as I mentioned, Jeff is doing this on a part-time basis. His full-time job is a fireman outside of Boston. He loves the freedom and flexibility this business provides him. The money he's making is just improving the quality of his life and ensuring that he'll be super comfortable when he retires from the fire department in a few years.

Step 4: Marketing

Once we have the properties, we now need to start bringing in more buyers than we can handle. This is such an important aspect of this business. You have to be vigilant about finding creative and inexpensive ways to market your property.

I'm going to pull the curtain up and show you how and where I market my properties to bring in more buyers than I can actually manage. I'm going to show you step by step how to build a massive buyers list so that you can even presell properties before you buy them.

In all my deals, I have never had a property that just sat there and didn't sell. Out of thousands of transactions, I've never lost money on a deal. How many businesses do you think can look at their inventory and say they never lost money on even one single item? Even Apple had a few duds before the iPod and iPhone. (U2 iPod, anyone?)

This is a pretty rare and special achievement I'm very proud of.

Plus, I'm a risk-averse guy. I'm the kind of guy who drives in the right-hand lane and doesn't make a move before considering everything.

When you combine the power of buying property for pennies on the dollar with a powerful marketing strategy, you have a sure fire formula for making money. That's what my marketing program is going to give you.

Once you have your marketing in place, there is only one step left. It's also my favorite step.

Step 5: Sell the Property (Close the Deal)

Now, I had a little bit of sales experience as an investment banker before getting into the land business. However, most of my students don't like sales. They think that salespeople need to be pushy or hyper aggressive to be effective. But here's the thing: sales is just the process of transferring your enthusiasm for land to another person.

That's it.

Here's an important idea to always keep in mind. If you're in this business just to make money for yourself, and not to provide value to your customers, then you will be sabotaging your long-term success.

Sure, you'll make money in the short run, but I guarantee it won't last. You have to have the attitude that you are in the business of creating new and better land solutions or investments for your customers. You need to have a mission and a sense of purpose. Ignore this advice, and your business will become soulless. Your customers will eventually see through you and realize that you're not looking out for their best interests.

Again, you can make short-term money doing this with the wrong attitude, but after a few years you'll still be scrambling for new customers instead of being able to simply send an email out to your past customers and get sales within minutes.

Unlike, housing, or any other real estate investing strategy, raw land already has a built-in best buyer. Do you know whom it is? Ok, think about... Fine, I'll just tell you—it's the neighbors. We get a list of the adjoining property owners from the county or online GIS maps and send out a a "neighbor letter".

The letter states that before we go to the open market, here is your opportunity to increase your land holdings, protect your views and know your neighbors. Often times, the neighbors end up buying first.

However, if they pass on the deal—let's talk about my

favorite marketing platforms. The second fastest way right now to sell land is by just putting it on Craigslist. Craigslist is in the top ten highest-traffic websites in the United States. I'm a big believer in platforms that already have traffic. I get so frustrated when my coaching students start spending money to build their own website.

You don't even need one. You can use platforms such as Craigslist, Facebook Buy-Sell Groups, eBay, Zillow, Landmodo.com, LANDFLIP.com, and LandWatch.com to market your property.

Look at a website such as LandWatch or Landsofamerica. com. These sites get about five hundred thousand people a month who are looking to buy land.

Now, if you have a piece of land and you know there's a platform such as Landmodo, don't you think that would be a good place for you to advertise your piece of land?

Absolutely. You want to be where your market is. You want to advertise where people are looking for what you're selling. Therefore, sites such as Landmodo, LANDFLIP, LandWatch, and Craigslist are the places you should focus on at first.

Eventually, you'll want to put up your own website. But in the beginning, I don't want you putting your energy and money into building a website. However, I do think you need a landing page or a squeeze page where your prospects can sign up to get updates and valuable information from you. This way, when they're ready to buy your property, they already know you and trust you. Later on, I'm going to share with you how you can get your own landing page or squeeze page for free.

All right, let's continue. Do you have debt? If you do, no worries. Let's solve that problem by making money to pay that off and get that debt gorilla off your back.

I didn't start out with much money—just $3,000—and my buddy Jeran had only $800. Most of my clients actually start out with little money in the bank. We can easily overcome this problem. I'm going to teach you how to lock up deals using lease options and how to flip these properties by wholesaling—all by using just a very small amount of money from your own pocket. I know what you're thinking, "how do I do this?"

You find a deal, lock up the property with a lease option for $0.20–$0.30 on the dollar, and then you immediately turn around and sell it for a quick profit. Whom do you sell it to? You sell it at a wholesale price to a retailer like me or someone from my network at a sizable discount from market value.

After buying the property for $0.20–$0.30 on the dollar,

you'll sell it for $0.60–$0.70 on the dollar. This way, you do what my Realtor friend Kathy Courtney likes to call "leaving some fat on the hog" for the retailer to make profits. It's a win-win deal for you (the wholesaler) and the retailer.

For example, you lock up a property worth $20,000 using an option. You have it under contract for $5,000. You flip it for $10,000 to a retailer and lock in a nice $5,000 profit for doing minimal work. If a property is really worth $20,000 and you sell it for $10,000, how many retailers do you think are going to be knocking on your door to buy that deal from you?

"Whoa, wait a minute, Mark. What if I lock up this property and nobody wants it?"

Well, think about it. If you lock up a property for $5,000 that's worth $20,000, do you really think you're going to lose money on that deal? Of course not! The real value is in locking up the deal and finding the seller.

This is the only business that I know of where the worst-case scenario is that you make a profit of 30–100 percent. The worst-case scenario in this example is you sell the property for $7,000 or $8,000, and you still make $2,000–$3,000 without putting a dime out of your own pocket. That's an infinite return on your investment. That's the key here.

Then you will take your profits and build a war chest of cash. That's exactly what I did. When I made my $12,000 off my first $3,000 invested, I took that money and reinvested it. Now, you could pay off some debt and then reinvest. So every deal I do, I take a little bit of the money and either reinvest in my business, add a virtual assistant, or increase my marketing budget.

You can do the same thing except now you can start paying off your debt. As long as you continue your deal flow, you'll start flipping properties again and again and again, and soon you'll have a war chest of cash and no debt.

"Mark, I've known some people who started in land, did a few deals, and then went on to do something else. Why is that?"

I can't speak for everyone, but I know that it's human nature that when something gets difficult, we can contract "shiny object syndrome." This is a behavior pattern where if someone doesn't achieve immediate success, they bail and move on to the next "shiny object," be it a different investing program or another business startup idea.

It gets frustrating sometimes, because I know land is the best passive income model. I've proven it over and over myself. My friends and business partners Scott Todd and Tate Litchfield have proven it over and over again. My students Jeff, Mike, Tom, Frank, and dozens of others have proven it over and over again. Just got to https://www.thelandgeek.com/student-success/ for example after example.

What can I say? It works.

The truth is, as in any endeavor in life, success takes time. It takes some struggle. You need to develop some stamina and be able to suffer a few defeats along your way to victory. You need to commit yourself to the learning curve of discovering what works for others, testing it out, and putting in the time.

"Mark, what traits do your most successful clients possess that others lack?"

Glad you asked. That's the focus of the next two chapters.

First, you need to possess (or if you don't possess it, then learn how to develop) the number one trait needed to be successful in land.

Second, you need to be able to do what I call embracing the suck.

Let's dive into the first trait.

Chapter 5

The Number One Trait Required for Success in Land (and Real Estate in General)

Do you love getting a good deal? I mean really love getting a good deal?

Are you the kind of person who "visits" an item in the store that you really want, waiting for that magical day when it's finally on sale before opening up your wallet?

Do you love telling the story of how you so frustrated the car salesman with your bargaining skills that he swore at you under his breath as he agreed to the offer that he said would "never be approved"?

Have you ever driven over an hour to visit an outlet mall, knowing that you can get the same items for almost half the price of your local department store?

If you answered yes to any or all of these questions, then you know the thrill of the chase. It's a rush, sometimes accompanied by a full-body shake, an ear-to-ear smile, and a shout of "Ha!" Then there may be a handful of fist pumps, high fives, and a little jig.

It's the joy of victory, knowing you're smarter than the average buyer who paid full price. It's the pride of a winner, knowing you outwitted the "system" and walked away with cash in your pocket.

Sometimes, this can get me into trouble as I lose sight of the value of my own time as I chase and chase the best possible deal. Nevertheless, getting the best deal possible is like a drug to me, and I'm definitely a deal junkie.

I stress this point because I truly believe that to be successful in the land business, you need to love (and when I say "love," I mean "live for") getting a good deal.

Think about it. Good deals are the basis of wealth for almost every business. You've likely heard the old axiom "Buy low, sell high." It's as true today as it was for the merchants who sold their wares from stalls in the agoras of Ancient Greece.

It's how Warren Buffett got rich. You can boil everything he did down to "buy low, sell high."

It's how Donald Trump got rich. He bought Manhattan property for pennies on the dollar, redeveloped it, and then raked in many times what he paid for it through a combination of buy-and-hold and sell strategies.

It's how Sam Walton built Walmart by buying in bulk and passing the savings on to the consumer who couldn't resist the deals.

I also received this lesson from my Dad who was a wholesale grocer.

"Put that down!" said my dad, referring to the stick of Wrigley's Spearmint gum in my hand. We were in line with my mother at the local supermarket.

"It's just gum, Dad," I said.

"They're charging a dollar here! I pay 40 cents for that same stick of gum, then sell it to the grocery store for 60 cents. There's no way a son of mine is going to pay a dollar for a stick of gum!"

Sheepishly, I placed the gum back into its spot on the shelf.

You can see where I get it from. My Dad's pride wouldn't let me buy that gum at full price. My Mom was the same way.

This dedication to paying less than retail was so ingrained in my Dad that he, to this day, refuses to buy anything without some sort of a discount. While I often went without gum due to my parents' obsession with bargain prices, they gave me a wonderful gift. It's one of the core investing principles I've adopted: don't overpay.

So why is this so important for success in business? I'm sure you've also heard the saying "Money is made on the buy." Again, ancient words of wisdom that still hold true today.

In order to sell a product or service, you need to get the cost of bringing that product or service to market as low as possible so you can make enough money when you sell it to the end consumer. This is what is commonly known as the margin. The higher the margin, the more profit.

Even if you create your own product, the price for which you sell it includes a markup that takes into account your cost of materials and time spent making it. If you struggle to make money selling products you make yourself, then likely you're (1) in a market in which there isn't enough demand for your product to make it profitable, or (2) you're spending too much to make the product in comparison to what the market will pay for it.

This is where a nose for a good deal comes in handy. If you didn't grow up with parents who picked up pennies in parking lots or clipped coupons from weekly mailers, then you may be at a disadvantage.

Call us deal junkies. Call us bargain hunters. Whatever. To make money, and especially to make money in real estate of any kind, you need to develop this joy of getting a good deal.

Or, as I like to call it, the thrill of the chase.

The great thing about learning how to become a bargain hunter who loves the thrill of the chase is that once you get it, you get it. It's burned into your psyche for life.

Once you make your first few hundred dollars flipping land, it's almost like a new personality emerges. Nothing looks the same. You begin to look for deals everywhere, for almost everything you buy.

When I was in my investment banker phase making cold calls, I got a handful of thrills at a handful of good deals. But it was hard, mind-numbing work. I hate to say it, but there were too many elements of it that made my soul sick.

While the notion of getting a good deal and the notion of taking calculated risky moves may seem diametrically opposed on the surface, they're actually not. My decision that day was fueled by my addiction to the high of buying something for pennies on the dollar.

I involuntarily gasped as Jeran and I pulled into the parking lot of the auction. It looked like the town Clint Eastwood rode into in *A Fistful of Dollars*, only with cars.

"Am I really doing this?" I asked myself.

On the way from the parking lot to the auction hall, I decided I was out. There was no way I was going to buy land in this desolate area. No way. I patted my checkbook, safe and sound in my shirt pocket. I'm just going to enjoy the trip, I told myself, and watch my pal make a fool of himself.

Forty-five seconds later when we walked into the auction hall, I decided I was back in.

The thrill of the chase fired up deep inside me when I saw that there was almost nobody in the auction room. There were about twenty locals, none of whom looked like they'd be a bidding threat. I expected to be greeted by a roomful of chubby "land sharks" in ten-gallon hats smoking big cigars, but when I saw my competition, my spirits got a well-needed boost.

"Let's begin," said the auctioneer.

My heart skipped a beat. I reached into my shirt pocket and lifted my checkbook an inch. The air was thick with the sweet smell of deals to be had.

The minimum bid was $150 and up for each half-acre parcel. We looked at only the lowest ones. I had already promised myself that there was no way in hell I was going to pay more than $300 for property in such a place as Deming, New Mexico.

My palms were sweaty. My heart beat out of my chest as I raised my hand. I decided, for such a low price, how can I possibly be hurt?

Right?

I mean, what's the worst that could happen?" I rationalized. Worst-case scenario, we own land. It's an asset. Nobody can destroy it. One day, maybe we'll be able to make a couple hundred bucks off it. Or, maybe I could just barter services for it. I'm thinking, free dentistry or haircuts for a year or two.

By the time the auction was over, I had bought a good chunk of raw land.

In Deming, New Mexico! Me! Mark Podolsky from Scottsdale now owns land he's never been to, never even seen.

Holy cow!

"What have I done?" I said to my friend, burying my face in my hands.

He just smiled at me and said, "Don't worry. You'll see."

We went to the assessor's office and bought plat maps for seventy-five cents. Then we took pictures of the surrounding area.

This was not stunning land. I mean, sure there were mountains in the distance, but it was mostly rocks and dirt. Lots of dirt.

The next day, with my hands shaking so much that I kept hitting the wrong keys on my IBM laptop, I placed my properties up for sale on eBay for a seven-day auction with a minimum bid of one lousy dollar.

All I could hear was my wife's voice dancing in my head saying, "Dammit, Mark, we needed that $3,000 for car repairs! How could you do this to me? To us?"

I bit my nails as the photo from my eBay auction went live. Wow, I'm really doing this, aren't I?

My wife's voice was right. We did need that $3,000 for car

repairs. What am I doing gambling like this? Suddenly, I felt like the guy who takes his family's life savings to put a giant stack of chips on twenty-two at the roulette table.

Luckily, that feeling didn't last long.

In thirty days, all ten parcels I bought sold. Not only did they sell, but they also sold for $1000 each plus a recording fee of $199. I just made a 300 percent return on my investment! That's $8,990 in pure sweet delightful profit!

I cannot fully describe the joy I felt. It was a high unlike any I had ever known. Like my birthday, anniversary, and graduation day all rolled into one.

I wanted to dance naked on rooftops. I wanted to howl at the moon. I wanted to kiss random strangers. (I did none of that, though. OK, well, maybe one of those. I'll never tell which one, so don't ask.)

I was hooked.

Bad.

It wasn't enough. I needed more. Like a junkie, I needed to experience this again. I would have sold my soul at that moment just to get to the next auction.

I had to wait only a month.

The room in southern Arizona a month later was even better than New Mexico. There were only about ten people in the room. I smiled at Jeran.

"Lock and load, buddy," I said with a gleam in my eye.

"I've created a monster," said my buddy.

This time, we were buying properties for as little as $5–$10. I bought about ninety of them.

Over the next six months, I sold all ninety properties. I made more than $92,000 just from that one auction.

Life would never be the same.

One Saturday morning while recovering from a particularly bad week at the investment firm, I poured a glass of orange juice. The baby was playing, and my wife was making pancakes.

I cleared my throat.

"Honey," I said, "I think I'm really onto something with this land stuff."

"I know," she said. "It's great." She opened the refrigerator door, took out a half gallon of milk, and added some to the pancake mix in the bowl.

I took a deep breath. "So I've decided to quit my job."

Has time ever slowed so much for you that it froze in place like an oil painting? That's what happened when my wife looked at me, the half gallon of milk still in her hand. The baby went still. There was no sound. A thousand years seemed to pass as she gave me a look that can only be described as equal parts bewilderment and anger. If you're married, you know the look.

"No," she said as time resumed its journey. She placed the milk back into the refrigerator. Whew, I thought she was going to throw it at me.

"No," I repeated.

She closed the refrigerator door and looked me in the eye again.

"Absolutely not," she said.

"Absolutely not," I repeated and sipped my orange juice.

Well, that was that.

Fast-forward eighteen months.

I'm still land flipping part time. I'm still a full-time miserable investment banker. Monday morning is worse than a trip to hell for me. My soul is empty. My spirit is anywhere but there, and I'm considering alcoholism.

There's one big difference, though.

My income from land flipping has just exceeded my income from the investment firm.

All because of the thrill of the chase, the number one trait required to be successful in land (or any real estate).

But that wasn't the only trait that fueled my success. I had also learned how to embrace the suck.

Chapter 6

Embrace the Suck: How to Not Lose Your Mind while Becoming Dirt Rich

———

"This could be yours," says the man in the straw hat and floral shirt. He sips from a huge round salt-rimmed glass with a long stem and a tiny green umbrella. Behind him, an immense mansion looms behind an outdoor swimming pool surrounded by decorative stone.

"And this!"

The television image pops to the same man in a tuxedo leaning on a red Ferrari with a stunning blonde woman in a black cocktail dress on his arm. She moves her hand to her round hip while pursing her lips and lowering her eyes as she stares into the camera.

"And the best part is," he says, now in an office sitting in front of a laptop, palm trees and an aquamarine bay outside the window, "you need to work only one hour a week!"

He turns his attention to the laptop, clicks the mouse once, and slams it shut. He leans back in his chair, folding his fingers behind his head.

"Done!" he says with a yawn. "Man, am I tired!"

OK, enough, right?

You know what I'm talking about. If you've been alive at all in the twenty-first century, you've seen late-night infomercial gurus peddling dreams of instant unlimited riches for almost no work.

Even the term *late-night infomercial* has almost no meaning anymore because these scam artists can be found 24/7 on the internet, promising untold wealth only if you buy their course for an outrageous fee in several easy installments.

Nowadays, it seems like almost anyone can set themselves up as a guru selling almost any made up BS, charge thousands for it, and attract a legion of followers based almost solely on their personality.

A huge chunk of this market is focused on real estate. This dates back to the early days of information products in the 1970s when smarmy get-rich-quick peddlers would sell cassette tapes through direct mail on how to buy houses for no money down.

It's only gotten worse since then, with hucksters promising riches while making real estate sound so easy. Just like taking a nap and then money arrives in your account.

Now, the truth is that when I nap, money does arrive in my account.

I also freely admit that sometimes in my marketing it can look easy, but that's only because I've been doing it for so long.

I promise you this: you'll never see me standing in front of a mansion promising you that the path to success is an easy straight line that requires no work.

True, once you do the work and set the machine up, your days get easier, even a lot easier. To get to that point, however, requires commitment, a sometimes-steep learning curve, and the mental strength to embrace the suck and push through the dips.

I'm blessed to have an easier life now, but to get here, I had to hit some brick walls, learn some hard lessons, and in many ways start over again several times.

One of my favorite books is Seth Godin's *The Dip*. It's a short book but packs a powerful message.

In almost every business venture (or almost any type of project really), things tend to start off swimmingly. There is a rise in productivity and even a couple of small wins may occur.

Then comes the dip. It's inevitable, nearly guaranteed. You're riding high on your initial small wins, putting in the same amount of effort, chugging along at full speed.

But nothing happens.

"Hmm, that's strange," you say to yourself. "I had a few small wins there." So you buckle down and push harder, putting in even more effort.

Still, nothing.

Welcome to the dip.

This is the true test of grit. It is at this point that winners break away from losers.

You are now faced with a choice: quit or press on.

If you suspect that your model is the problem, then quitting may be a good idea. As I write this in 2018, if your major competitor is Amazon.com, quitting is probably a good choice. At this moment, Amazon is guaranteed to win. It will smoke you. Time to find something else.

However, if you know from your research and conversations with reputable people that you have a proven business model, quitting is a terrible idea. You are so close to bigger wins, if only you tough it out just a little longer.

The dip is a test. A tease. It demands you prove your worthiness by kicking you in the teeth just to see how you'll react.

Don't let the dip beat you. Go the distance, stay on your feet, and you will learn the most powerful lesson in business.

On the other side of the dip flow thundering rewards like nothing you've ever seen before. It's like a gushing waterfall of success, hitting you so hard that you're barely prepared for it.

Once you emerge on the other upward side, you are often faced with a series of new problems, all related to managing the new inflow of activity produced by all your actions during the dip.

When I first read Godin's book, I laughed out loud because I know it is so true. Not only have I experienced the dip myself, but I've also witnessed it with my coaching students time and time again.

The path to success is a squiggly line. Up, down, bigger up, bigger down, even bigger up, even bigger down, and so on.

Everybody hits rough patches. What makes people successful is their resiliency. The ones who, faced with a dip, get back up again and continue the fight are the ones who reap the true rewards.

A fantastic book devoted solely to this subject, is Angela Duckworth's best selling book titled Grit: The Power of Passion and Perseverance.

As I said, it's important that you know what you're doing has a chance at succeeding. If you read the comments from my students and watch some of the amazing testimonial videos they've made, you'll see that land investing is the best passive income model in the world.

(I'm open to anyone who has a better one. I even hosted a podcast for a year where I invited people to challenge my model. So far, I've found nothing better.)

As you begin, you're probably going to have a small win or two. That's the time to mentally prepare yourself for the dip that's on its way.

Then, once you get past your first dip, don't rest on your laurels. It's important to know that there's an even bigger dip (with an equal reward) on its way.

One of my students, John, experienced this. He bought the investor's toolkit, learned everything in it backward and forward, started mailing, and bought a property.

Then he listed it for sale. Nothing. He posted ads. Nothing. He posted more ads.

Weeks went by but nothing.

He came to boot camp looking for answers. He went home, retooled his strategy, and doubled down.

Another month went by and nothing.

John knew he was working with a good model, though. He had met too many people having so much success in the land business to doubt that this does work. He knew he just had to keep pushing through this dip.

Then overnight, everything changed. A buyer contacted John, immensely thrilled about the property. It was just what he had been looking for. Two easy payments via a program called geekpay.io and a simple recording later, John was in business as a land investor.

Another student of mine, Fred, owned twenty properties. Fred had a bit more experience and had accumulated some great land at some very low prices.

The problem was, they weren't selling. Fred got frustrated. He developed shiny object syndrome and began looking elsewhere for his business model. He bought forex programs, house flipping programs, and tax lien investing programs.

Worst of all, Fred stopped locating new properties. He lost faith in the proven model, so his land business stood still.

Then, in one week, ten of Fred's properties sold. He went from making $200 a month in passive income to $1,400 almost overnight.

The next week, five more properties sold, bringing Fred's monthly passive income up to $1,800 a month.

"You were so right, Mark," he told me on a Voxer message. "I should have just stuck with it. I was such an idiot to quit."

Fred's next problem was that he was low on inventory or what I call deal flow. (More on that in the next chapter.) Any business, whether you're selling coffee or lumber, isn't a business if it has no inventory. The same is true for land. If you have no land to sell, then you have no land business.

Fred learned the hard way to never stop finding new deals, because every piece of land will eventually sell.

I say this with 99.9 percent certainty because since 2001, I have never—as in not once, not ever—been unable to sell a parcel of land.

As I'm fond of saying, "There's a pig for every barn."

True, you may have to embrace the suck and wait a while for that pig to find the barn you're selling, but the two will eventually find each other.

Heck, even I still have dips. Nobody is immune. True, I can weather them better now because (1) I have a momentum built over the years and (2) experience has taught me how to handle a large variety of situations.

Having survived many dips, my momentum generates

a base of wealth that acts as a "cushion," able to absorb the impact of a financial hit better than someone just starting out.

Even as I write this, I'm hitting a dip caused by a heady stream of new properties entering my pipeline. Too much land is coming in. It's overwhelming the virtual assistants I've hired to process all of it. Sometimes too much of a good thing is a brick wall. True, it's a good problem to have, but it's still a problem.

Another advanced problem is people who default. Just recently, two people suddenly stopped paying me in one month. I truly hate when that happens.

I always try to work with people, to find out if there's a problem I can help them solve. These two, however, just vanished. Gone, just like that. Not returning phone calls, heads stuck in the sand.

And both were so close to paying off their notes. That's the sad part. The land could have been theirs in just a few more months.

After giving them time to get back to me and hopefully resolve the situation, I had to take the only option available to me: resell the properties.

I like people, especially people I've built a relationship with, but this is business. Others with not as much heart as me may celebrate the fact that they can now resell a property and earn a truly unbelievable return on investment from this default, but I can't help but feel bad about it.

Now I must accept the fact that my note portfolio just shrank by two monthly payments. I may lose two more months if I don't resell it fast as well.

So I know that all I can do is embrace the suck by executing my land contract and ending the note, then getting those properties back into the marketing funnel.

The truth is that this has happened so many times now that I've built it into my income projections. I know that every single month a certain percentage of my passive income is just going to disappear and I need to be prepared for it.

When you're prepared for coming dips, you can weather them much easier.

Here's another favorite quote of mine:

Every great story on the planet happened when someone decided not to give up, but kept going no matter what. Spryte Loriano

If you can embrace the suck and weather each dip, solving problems and automating systems, eventually you actually can live life on your own terms.

Automation is key to this. It may just be my favorite word. I teach land investors how to set everything up so it's running without you. Your systems are all in place, doing the work for you.

While I do love automation so much that I teach students how to implement it early in their business, you can't do what some students try to do: buy their way out of experiencing dips.

In the beginning as you scale up, it's important that you actually feel the frustration of the dip and the necessity to embrace the suck.

What happens if you accelerate too fast? The wheels on your bus start to shake. That's why it's a good idea to make sure the wheels are rolling straight before accelerating to a hundred miles an hour.

Once you're sure your bus can handle this speed, that's when to flip the automation switch. It's great to ramp up, but just make sure your systems can support it. Embracing the suck is the only proven way to do this.

Embracing the suck comes down to daily effort.

If you're not making some sort of daily effort in your business to move the needle, then the dip will surround and destroy you.

My good friend and fellow Land Geek coach Scott Todd called this focusing on the controllables.

You can't control what other people do. You can't control whether they're going to buy your property. You can't control whether a seller is going to accept your offer.

However, you can control what you do. This is how you measure your success. It may be a leap of faith at first, but if you focus on just what you can control, the results will absolutely definitely come.

Focusing on your controllables also helps you to keep your emotions in check.

Ask yourself these questions:

Did I do county research today?

Did I make my target number of offers today?

Did I price my properties right today?

Did I provide top-notch customer service today?

Did I do proper due diligence today?

Did I place enough property ads today?

If you answered all these questions positively, then you know you have so much activity going on that any one problem won't throw your entire business into a tailspin.

The worst decisions I've ever made were emotional decisions based on fear and panic. They never turned out well.

The way around this is to know that your daily effort is so strong that you have several fallbacks in the works. You're creating so much forward momentum that no single problem is going to stop you dead in your tracks.

It's a one-to-one ratio between effort and results in this business.

The choice is yours.

Will you remain mired in fear? Or will you quickly dust yourself off, get back out there, and double down?

If you've read this far, then I think I know the type of person you are.

Let's talk about deal flow.

Chapter 7

Deal Flow: The Lifeblood of Your Business

One of the highlights of my week is the day I open my mail live on Facebook. I'm joined by several Land Geek coaching students, land enthusiasts, and opportunity seekers.

It's such a thrill to turn on my camera, greet everyone, and dive into the day's stack of mail. Completely unrehearsed, I open each envelope and react to what's inside.

On a typical Wednesday, I open an envelope and find my offer sent back to me with a magic marker scrawl:

Don't insult me! This property is worth $35,000! F%^&you!

I laugh and toss it in the trash. My offer for the property was $1,100 because comps (comparable sales) average $4,400. That's how much I know I can make if I sell it on terms. (Yes, that's a 300 percent return. Pretty common in this business. More on that later.)

The next letter is a counteroffer. I offered $750, and they are willing to sell to me for $1,000.

This one I might accept. Usually, I'll start due diligence on the property and find something that allows me to negotiate down to very close to my actual offer price. If not, $1,000 isn't bad for a property I know will sell for $9,500 on easy financing terms.

The next letter is another nasty insult. Goes with the territory. This is business. The only way to buy low is to make insanely low offers. Property owners tend to take easy offense to these, so you need to learn to ignore it. They stopped bothering me many years ago.

The next letter is a signed acceptance. No note. Nothing but a signature on my offer. This is the best possible scenario. If your county research is solid, your offer is not too high or too low, and you're mailing high volume, then you, too, will receive a signed offer almost every day, hidden in there among the offended.

It's worth it.

Because I know that one signed offer is going to make me at least a couple of thousand dollars. Easy. Usually a lot more.

So do people just mail offers to me because I'm Mark Podolsky, the Land Geek?

I wish it were that simple. To get that many responses, I mail a lot. Not that I ever see it anymore because the system is so automated, but every week several hundred offers get mailed to tax-delinquent property owners.

(I know you have questions. Don't worry, I will soon detail the exact process I use so that you can replicate it yourself.)

You're also probably thinking, "That's a lot of postage."

Yes, it is, but it's nothing compared to the money I get back.

OK, let's back up a bit. How do we locate distressed properties?

First things first. Let's talk about county research.

County Research

This is the most important critical step when first starting out. If you don't know (1) where to mail and/or (2) how much to offer, then you aren't going to make any money.

In my investor's toolkit, I outline the best counties in which to invest. This is a list based on my years of experience in this business. I know where the best deals are to be had because I've tested so many counties since 2001.

(To get your copy of the investor's toolkit, visit here: www. thelandgeek.com/training

In the meantime, I can tell you that I've had by far the greatest success in the southwestern United States and Florida.

The first thing you need to do is pick a county and start your research.

First, you want to check to see if there's any buying and selling activity in this county.

"Mark, shouldn't I be looking for a county where there are no sales, where I will have no competition?"

No. You actually want to do the opposite. You want to go where everybody else is buying and selling right now.

I know this appears counterintuitive, but you will soon realize that it's not.

There's an old saying: "Only pioneers get arrows in their backs."

You want to be buying and selling land in an area where there is a demand for land. There is a demand for land in areas where there are a lot of sales. For some reason or another right now, that area is booming. That's where you want to be.

What is the best way to find out where there are a lot of sales? Well, as you may well know, all real estate transactions are a matter of public record. You could go county by county and do painstaking research to find out where land is selling.

But there's a much easier way.

There are a ton of websites that list land for sale. I'm talking a ridiculous number of them. Two of the most well-known are:

Landandfarm.com
Landwatch.com

Both have been around for years. On top of that, there are many, many others.

Right now, just for fun, go to Google. Type in a state name and the word *land*. For example, "Arizona land." Then, hit Enter.

See what I mean? I just did it, too. As of this writing, here's what Google displayed:

landmodo.com (my personal favorite)
landandfarm.com
landwatch.com
blueskiesland.com
billyland.com
landsofarizona.com
landflip.com
arizonaland.com
landcentury.com
landforgood.org

Depending on when you're reading this, the results will be different. Some sites will close, but new ones will spring up because there are hundreds of thousands of people—maybe even millions—whom buy land.

This can be a mind-altering concept for many newbies to this business, mainly because you don't hear about the land business very often in the news or entertainment media. Even in business news, you don't hear about very many land deals. The vast majority of people in the United States are bombarded with tech company news to the exclusion of many other, nearly hidden industries.

Hey, nothing wrong with that. I love tech. (I am a "geek," after all.) If there's a new app that can improve my life by 0.01 percent, I'm usually the first person I know to download it to my iPhone and test it out.

But there's a lot more going on out there business-wise than new Apple or Amazon products. Quietly in the background, there are a lot of people making a lot of money in various ways.

As I've already stated, I believe land is the best investment, the best passive income business, and the best business—period. But it's not typically "sexy," so TMZ isn't talking about it. Neither is Drudge, the Huffington Post, CNN, or Fox News.

Luckily for us, you won't flip to HGTV or the DIY network and see me in front of my computer hosting "Flipping Land." It's an unsexy niche. In fact, go to your local REIA meeting (Real Estate Investor Association) and if there are are 100 people in the room 99 of them will be house flippers, landlords, or home wholesalers. You and I would be the only land investors.

But take a stroll through the land websites you find in your Google search and you will see how vast the market for land in the United States is. It's one of the reasons I'm not afraid to share all I know about this business. It's so vast that there truly is enough business to keep us busy and lucrative for the rest of our lives if we work it right.

Don't make the mistake of just casually visiting these sites. Spend time there. See where there are the most listings. Take notes. You will soon start to recognize patterns. You will begin to see the matrix of where the most activity is.

Truth is, activity changes year to year. One year, a county in Arizona was the hottest place. The next year, it was one in Nevada. The next year, it might be in Colorado.

The market is constantly changing, which is why you need to continually perform this research. I still have my team do this every week. Even with all my years of experience, I'm not a fortune teller. What worked last year may not be the best investment this year. What's a windfall this year may be a dud next year.

Once you have your list of counties where there's a lot of activity, it's time to create your plan.

Let's suppose you've decided to start mailing offers to Mosquito County, Florida.

Here's a simple way one of my coaching students does it. Open up an Excel spreadsheet and make a list of properties for sale there. Group them into columns:

List Date – Town – Subdivision – Acres – Price – Terms or Cash – APN – Source

Fill in as much information as you can for each property:

List Date: This is just so you know when you recorded this information. Six months from now, prices may have changed. You want to ensure that your information is current as well as be able to notice trends over time.

Town: This is good information to know, just as a reference point if nothing else. Sometimes one town in a county might be priced differently than another.

Subdivision: Same as town. Many properties are not even in a town or subdivision, but if they are, this helps your research.

Acres: Next, group everything by acreage. You may want to cluster one- to two-acre properties together, three to five acres, five to ten acres, and so forth.

Price: The amount the seller is asking for the property on the land sites. (*Note*: As in residential real estate, this amount can vary widely from the final selling price. Forget that for now. We're only establishing a baseline idea for the amount that properties are selling in this area.)

Terms or Cash: This is important information to know. Properties priced to sell for cash are typically lower. If the seller is owner financing it, the total over time is almost always much higher. (Another reason the land business is the best passive income model.)

For your purposes, you need to decide whether you're going to be selling for cash or terms. In the long run, terms is much more profitable. I rarely, if ever, sell for cash. If you're starting out on a budget, however, selling for cash is a good way to grow your investment fund with an eye to eventually owner finance all your sales. However, another strategy is to sell all your properties on easy financing terms and if you need cash just sell 12 months of payments to an investor on a site like www.tlfolio.com. You then get your principal out to reinvest in another deal, and have that passive income boomerang back to you 12 months later.

APN: This is the acronym for assessor's parcel number, the standard reference number for land parcels in the United States.

Source: The website from which you got this information. This is good to know because sometimes you may notice that some sites are priced higher than others.

Once you've collected all the data from the sites you found, add up the totals, then divide by the number of properties you have. That's how you find the median selling price for that county.

For example, on your Excel spreadsheet, which contains properties that are one to two acres, let's say you have fifty-four of them. Add up all the prices listed and divide by fifty-four. That's your median sale price.

That's the price that, for our purposes, we are deciding a similar property will sell.

But what we want to know right now is how much we want to buy it for. Remember, buy low, sell high. Money is made when you BUY real estate.

Here is my top secret, classified, for-your-eyes-only, don't-tell-anyone—wink, wink—Land Geek superduper pricing formula:

Take the median price and divide by four. That gives us what Warren Buffet would call a "300% margin of safety."

Yep, that's it. Whew, tough, huh?

So, for example, if the median price of one- to two-acre properties in Mosquito County is $4,000, then your offer price becomes $1,000.

I know what you're thinking: why would anyone sell a property that's worth $4,000 for $1,000?

This concept stops many potential land investors dead in their tracks. They cannot wrap their heads around the fact that people would sell their land for less than its value, much less a full quarter of its value.

The truth is that there are so many reasons why a person would sell land for a quarter of its value.

Here are just a few:

- They inherited the land and don't care about it.
- They invested in an area that had a ton of potential for growth in a previous era but turned out to be a bust, and now they just want to stop paying back taxes.
- They're in financial difficulty, and even a quarter of the land's value would be a boon to them right now.

I could go on. I've heard so many stories throughout the years.

Bottom line is, they want to get rid of it. Some will give it away.

Why don't they sell it on their own? Because selling can be hard. Sometimes it's easy if you're in the right area, but often it's a tedious process. These people are paying attention to their jobs, their work, their children. They don't have time to learn everything we know about getting top dollar for land. And they certainly don't want to do notes. They want cash.

You make more money from notes (owner financing) than from cash, which is why this business is so lucrative. But most people don't want to hassle with the details of owner financing. In reality, even after all these years, most people don't even know owner financing exists, much less how to implement it.

The other reason to divide by four is that it leads us to a 300 percent return. That's the amount we usually want to strive for. Sometimes it will be a little less. Sometimes it will be a lot more. (I routinely sell parcels for a 1,000 percent return. You read that right. One thousand percent! I told you this is the best investment model ever. Where can you make 1,000 percent on your money? The stock market? The roulette wheel? No way!)

Now that you're armed with how you're going to approach

tax delinquent property owners in this county, it's time to get a list.

This is the next piece of the puzzle that stumps most people. But you're not most people because you're reading this book and I'm arming you with knowledge that 99 percent of the general population has no clue about. Plus, I have faith in you.

Getting a List

So, you now have your list of comps (comparable sales) and your offer price for Mosquito County, Florida.

Next, go to the website for Mosquito County, Florida. Scroll to the county treasurer (sometimes the tax collector in certain states).

Find the email address of the treasurer and send an email. Here's an example of what to send:

Dear Treasurer,

I'm interested in obtaining a list in Excel format (.csv or .xlsx) of all real property in your county that is currently delinquent for not paying their property taxes.

Sincerely,
Mark Podolsky

This list, also known as the delinquent tax roll, is your own personal gold mine. These are people who are most likely to want to sell their land.

Why? Because they already owe back taxes on it. That's a sure sign that they just don't care about it anymore. Many would just give it away to be done with the annual tax bill.

That's why you're targeting this list. You want to help these people out of their misery by offering money for something that they're already losing money on.

Get it? See how a lowball offer really isn't an insult? Many of my coaching students start out skittish about making such low offers. But when you're dealing with desperate sellers who just want to be rid of a tax bill, any offer is a good offer.

Once the county assessor/tax collector sends you the list, it's time to start your letter writing campaign.

As I've mentioned before, there are a handful of ways to find distressed properties. I told you the story of how I started by finding properties at a tax deed auction. Eventually, I found that a letter writing campaign was far superior.

In this chapter, we're going to look at the letter writing campaign. It is by far my favorite method. Why? Because it's the most lucrative in terms of your time and investment. Plus, you don't need to leave your computer to do it.

Here's what you're going to do: prepare an offer letter to all these people who owe back taxes.

I'm not the only land investor who will advise you to use this process. However, there is a huge difference in the method I teach and that of others.

Most other land investors will tell you it's a good idea to write a letter that basically says:

> *Hey,*
>
> *We're interested in your property. Go to our website http:// www... Put in your name and email address, and we'll send you an offer.*
>
> *Sincerely,*
> *Land Investor Joe*

(Land Investor Joe is not a real person, so don't assume I'm talking about anybody in particular.)

Land Investor Joe's goal here is for them to contact him, and guess what? They immediately find themselves on a mailing list.

I completely disagree with this approach. Here's the way I look at it:

I'm NOT in the negotiation business.

I'm NOT in the appraisal business.

I AM in the OFFER business.

I want to deal only with MOTIVATED SELLERS.

The "Take It or Leave It" Offer

Here's an example of a letter I might send out:

Go to www.thelandgeek.com/dirtrich for the download-able PDF and other resources.

As you can see, there is no invitation to talk on the phone. Yes, there is a line for counteroffers, but this is pretty much a "take it or leave it" letter. That's exactly how I want it to be.

You may use this letter or adapt one of your own. Once you do, you need to figure out whom to mail it to following everything I've recommended thus far.

Scrubbing a List

So you have a list. You've contacted the county, and they've sent you a huge .csv (comma delimited) spreadsheet file.

You're excited. You can't wait to start mailing. You download and open the file in Excel.

Take a deep breath. This is a defining moment in your land career. This is where the amateurs separate from the pros.

Why the melodrama here? Because staring at you is possibly the ugliest, most confusing thing you have ever seen in your entire life. It's a beast full of numbers, codes, amounts, property descriptions, addresses, names, and various symbols you don't recognize.

You may want to reread chapter 6, "Embrace the Suck," once you click on the file and see your first list because you're probably going to feel much like the poor guy on *Star Trek* who opened the box and looked at the alien ambassador who was so ugly he caused humans to go insane.

Fear not. You will not go insane. Yes, this is going to be work. Yes, you do need to learn how to do it. There are no shortcuts in life. You either dedicate yourself to what needs to be done and learn it, or you don't. It's your choice.

There is good news, though. Once you learn how to scrub one list, you can scrub any list. It takes only one or two times and you're a list scrubbing genius, ready to pass it on to your hired virtual assistant.

But I get ahead of myself. You need to do it at least one time yourself. You need to understand it before you can hire someone else to do it.

List scrubbing can be made easy or it can be made hard depending on your approach to it. Let's go back to the moment you see your first tax delinquent list.

You're likely shouting, "I'm done! Done with this business! I don't get it!"

Breathe. Count to ten. There is a magic phrase for what you need at this moment. (No, not an adult beverage.) The magic phrase is

Excel skills.

Although, to be quite honest, I'm not a big fan of that phrase. The phrase I truly love is

Someone else's Excel skills.

Like I said, when you're first starting out, you need to

do things yourself, but only up to a point. You will soon discover (and I do mean really soon) that list scrubbing is best handled by Excel experts.

But maybe you're an Excel expert yourself. Maybe VLOOKUP is as much part of your daily routine as breakfast cereal. If so, then great. List scrubbing may be something you can handle without breaking a sweat.

But if you're like most people, you're probably not an Excel Jedi Knight. Luckily for us, there is a virtual army out there waiting for us to hire them to do our dirty work.

Later, I'll talk more about automation, my favorite word. For now, just scrub that first list (or if it's really big, at least part of it) yourself, and then think about hiring someone else to work it for you.

You can go to Fiverr.com, where for $5 you can get a ridiculous number of things done. Just search for "Excel" and voilà! There's your army of Excel Jedis.

Or you could go to Upwork.com and hire an actual virtual assistant. You can easily find someone in the Philippines or Indonesia with great Excel skills for $3–$5 an hour.

Regardless of your beliefs about globalization, prudent businesses take advantage of great deals wherever they may be located. There isn't an iPhone or Mac that isn't made in China. It's just the way the world works. Wherever skilled labor is cheapest and available is the place to outsource it.

Perhaps there is someone in your local community or social circle who is an Excel Jedi. Post on Facebook what you're looking for, and you may be surprised to find that your veterinarian's daughter can scrub your list like nobody's business.

"I don't know, Mark," you may be thinking. "I think I'll just do it myself."

You may want to give it a go, but every student who has ever said that to me has eventually hired someone else to do it. Every single one.

Think about it. You're basically paying yourself $3 an hour if you do it yourself. Are you currently being paid $3 an hour? I sincerely doubt it. Would you accept $3 an hour for any type of work? I sincerely doubt that, too. The truth is, it is much more efficient to outsource this aspect of your business. Once you learn how to do it, hire someone to do it for you. Trust me, it's worth it.

So back to your new list of tax delinquent property owners. This is what to do with it.

First, open up a new Excel spreadsheet. Create the following columns:

APN
Owner's Name
Address
City
State
Zip
Parcel Size
Land Use Code

These are pretty much all you need to put together your first mailing. We've covered everything here except for Land Use Code. Typically, all delinquent property will be coded VL, Vacant Land, or a similar variation.

"Wait, Mark. Hold on. Don't I need to know the amount of back taxes owed? Isn't that important?"

Yes, it's important. But no, you don't need them at this point. Again, I need to make this clear: at this point.

Only when you get an accepted offer is it a good idea to look at back taxes. Right now, looking up all the back taxes due for each and every property in your offer mailing is a big waste of your time. In an ideal mailing, only 3–5 percent of property owners who receive your offer will respond. If you spend all your time weeding out back taxes that are too high (even in some cases worth more than the property itself), then you're wasting your time. Better just to mail and deal with it only when you get an offer back.

I can't stress this enough. I've seen many a land business career derailed by too much research up front. Do not do too much research on the front end! This is a huge mistake land newbies make all the time.

Remember earlier I said that at this stage, we are in the offer business, not the appraisal business. If you overanalyze properties now, you are wasting time. There is a time to appraise, but it comes only after you've received an offer. Note also that just because I made an offer doesn't mean that's the price I'm going to pay. If the back taxes are too high, I'm going to renegotiate.

The offer letter is only the starting point of a negotiation. I always include a line that says "Counteroffer: _____." If it's within reason, I'll call up the person and negotiate.

"But, Mark, didn't you say you aren't in the appraisal business?"

True, I'm not. But I *will* get on the phone right away with someone who accepts an offer.

The important thing is to get offers out the door. Mail them. Get them in the hands of potential sellers. Then deal with issues when they come in. I do know the taxes are delinquent. I just don't pay attention to how much at this point.

Now, what if the codes on the tax delinquent list are confusing? There is no uniform code across the United States. Every county has its own classification system. Many are similar, but some look like hieroglyphics.

When in doubt, call the assessor's office and ask, "Do you have a master data record that shows me what all these codes mean?" Never be afraid to pick up the phone and call someone. Not only are you getting the information you need, but you are also building relationships with the people who work in the counties.

"Mark, what if I end up mailing to someone who owes more taxes than the property is worth?"

Yes, that could happen. Like I said, deal with it if and when it happens. And when it does, you just pass on that deal knowing that deals are like the bus. There is another one rolling down the road if you just a wait a few minutes.

Bottom line: nothing happens unless you're mailing. Mailing is the lifeblood of your business. If you're not mailing, then you're a chicken restaurant with no chicken.

The time to be an appraiser is not when you're mailing. The time to be an appraiser is when you have the offer back.

So back to your list. You've separated the data into columns. Now it's time to get rid of:

Duplicate owners
Other land investors
Out-of-country owners

Why out-of-country owners? Because it's a grind. I want things to be smooth. No translators or foreign laws to deal with. The last thing I need is an injunction from Her Majesty's barrister in a white wig because my offer violates UK law.

"But, Mark, I'm still unsure of my offer price."

I have good news for you. There are no set fixed prices in land. They're all over the place. It all comes down to the landowner and how much they are willing to accept. That's it. End of story. In fact, this is what makes our model so phenomenal. The market is completely inefficient.

Mailing Your Offers

Are you excited? You should be because it's time to mail. Mailing is the lifeblood of your business.

There are direct mail services you can use, such as click-2mail.com and others.

Or you could do as many of my Land Geek students do and use our proprietary software system LGPASS (Land Geek Proprietary Software Solution) that automates 90% of the business including the mailings. Just go to www.thelandgeek.com/training to learn more about this program.

You could handwrite your envelopes, which makes for a personal feel, or you can get a box of window envelopes from your local big-box store and line them up with your return and mailing addresses.

If you have kids, you could do what one student does and pay them ten cents per stuffed envelope with a stamp ready to go.

An easy way of getting started in this business is to take it one bite at a time. A good rule of thumb in the beginning is twenty in the box.

Several of my students have used this simple mantra to mail out thousands of offers. Why twenty? Because it's manageable.

Seriously, who can't get twenty offers in the mail every day? Without automation, you can do it in less than an hour. (With automation, you can do it in less than a minute.)

Twenty offers a day is also good because it gives you a solid hundred offers out a week. Looking at things in chunks of one hundred helps to evaluate your response rate.

For example, if you mail one hundred and the next week you get back three acceptances, you know you're doing well because you have a 3 percent response rate. (A 3–5 percent response rate is a good target.)

If your response rate is 0–2 percent, then there is a problem. Your offer amount may be too low. Problems are not a bad thing because they tell you what to do next week.

Remember, it's all about testing. Test, test, test. This applies to almost any business. Understand that it's going to take time, investment, and some sweat equity to find the right county and right offer that make your sweet spot.

Whatever you do, never stop mailing!

That is by far the number one biggest mistake I see my students make time and time again. I have so many voice messages from even some semi-advanced investors who say, "Mark, I was doing great and stopped mailing because

I was so busy. Now, everything has dried up, and I feel like I'm starting over."

Don't let this happen to you. Does Starbucks stop getting shipments of coffee just because they're too busy? No, because they're in the coffee business. They can't afford to run out of coffee because then they wouldn't be a coffee shop.

Same applies to you. If you're in the land business, you need inventory. Your product is land.

"But, Mark, what if it doesn't sell?"

I can honestly tell you that since I started buying land in 2001, I've bought a few clunkers. All of them sold. As in 100 percent of them.

Some of these parcels were really bad. I'm talking really stinky bad ugly hidden in valleys of death and covered in mud. Back in the early days, sometimes I would perform my due diligence without the expertise I have now and end up with some truly bad parcels. I didn't make a lot of money when I sold them, but I made some. But my point is that each and every one of them sold.

I cannot guarantee your experience, but I can tell you that the fear of being stuck with a piece of land is an irrational fear. Not one of my students has ever not been able to sell eventually, no matter how bad the parcel.

So how do you avoid even going near a bad property? Due diligence is the answer.

Chapter 8

Know Thy Property: The Due Diligence Checklist

So congratulations! You have an accepted offer. You're busting at the seams. You want to run shirtless through a field shouting, "I'm a real land investor, baby!"

Not so fast. You have some work to do. Now you need to ask yourself two important questions:

Is this really the best amount to pay for the property?

Is this truly a good deal?

Let's look at each of these questions to understand the importance of due diligence.

First: "Is This Really the Best Amount to Pay for This Property?"

If you determine that it isn't, then you need to adjust your offer price.

"Wait a minute, Mark. I already made an offer. Are you telling me to go back on my own word? Isn't that sleazy?"

No, not at all. Here's why: remember that in your carefully worded offer letter, you included phrases to protect yourself such as "outstanding property taxes within reason" and a list of contingencies. You may want to go back and review it now at www.thelandgeek.com/dirtrich.

By rescinding or revising an offer, you're only doing what you agreed to do. You may discover that the property is located in a remote area with no access that requires climbing a mountain to get there. That would significantly lower the land's value. (Notice I say "lower" because like I said before, all parcels sell eventually. There's a pig for every barn.)

Another example: you receive a signed acceptance offer for $700. You begin due diligence and see that according to the county treasurer's website the property owner owes $3,840 in back taxes.

Stop! That deal immediately becomes a pass. The taxes

owed are much higher than the actual value of the property. Very bad.

Let's say the tax amount owed is a less serious amount such as $250. Now you're in a much better position. You're not going to pay what you originally offered because it clearly states in the offer that you will only accept outstanding taxes within reason. Now you can renegotiate the offer price.

Call up the owner and say, "I've discovered that you owe $250 in back taxes. That means that I need to subtract that amount from my offer, so unfortunately I'm able to pay only $550 for the property instead of the $700 originally offered."

Sometimes they'll say no. Most times they'll see that you are their only way out and they'll say yes.

Another example: the person who signed the acceptance is the son or daughter of the owner to whom you mailed your offer, acting as the executor of the will of the now deceased owner.

If you're working in a state where the law requires that a property goes through probate before it can be resold, then your best option is to pass. Some states are easier than others to work with on this as they will accept an affidavit of heirship to avoid a costly quiet title action or probate issue. Consult an attorney or visit rocketlawyer. com for legal advice regarding your particular state.

Let's look at the second question.

"Is This Truly a Good Deal?"

Due diligence may uncover the fact that your property is part of an HOA (home owners' association) or POA (property owners' association). That can be a huge hassle to deal with and may cost you a small fortune in fees. (I generally advise students to stay away from these, although a handful of students have had some success with them.)

Due diligence may uncover the fact that the property is located between two rocky mesas, accessible only by an all-terrain vehicle (ATV), not to mention the only county-maintained road is eight miles away and to get to the parcel, you need to trespass on other people's properties.

Truth is, I've made a few dollars selling properties like these to rugged outdoor enthusiasts who love life way off the grid. One of my students sold one to a paleontologist looking for dinosaur bones.

You just need to ask yourself, "Do I want to deal with the

hassle of this property?" It may take a longer time to sell, and you may not make as much money as you would by focusing on other ones. It's up to you.

There was one time that I failed to do due diligence on a parcel I bought. I could have kicked myself when I saw that I had bought the side of a mountain, nearly vertical.

"Oh well," I thought, "just going to have to sell it for cheap." As a result, I listed it for sale on eBay.

Much to my surprise, a bidding war began. The amount kept going up and up and up over the course of the ten-day auction. I actually made a lot of money on that deal.

I got the buyer on the phone to do the closing, but I was uneasy. Unsure I could sleep soundly that night without bringing it up, I asked him, "You do know what you bought, right?"

"What do you mean?" he said.

"This property is on the side of a mountain. I just want to make sure you know."

"Oh yeah, I know," he said.

"Oh whew. That's a relief. Are you a mountain climber?"

"No, I'm a film director. The fees to shoot in the valley outside Hollywood are ten times more than the price of this property, so I'd rather buy it and shoot out there. It's a western."

I was floored!

See, when it comes to land, you just never know.

The Due Diligence Checklist

What are you looking for when performing your due diligence?

First, you need a copy of the deed. If you're working in a county with an easily accessible web platform, you may be able to just type in the APN (assessor's parcel number) and see a pdf of it. If not, then call the county assessor and have them email you a copy of it.

Once you have the deed, the most important piece of information you need to verify is that the name of the person on the deed is the person who agreed to sell you the property. If not, then you have a problem.

Like I mentioned earlier, the legal issues are different in every state, so consult an attorney or rocketlawyer.com. However, when you know the person is actually the owner of the property, then you know you're dealing with the right person.

Next, you want to make sure the title is clean. That means that there are no liens or claims against the owner of the property for any reason. Again, this information is available from the assessor.

(Tip: As your business grows, you may want to consider subscribing to homeinfomax.com. This is a great service that provides a wealth of information about almost any property in the United States, including a full history of liens and deeds.)

You also want to get from the assessor (or the assessor's website if available):

GPS coordinates: The exact latitude and longitude of the property.

Legal description: This is usually a long description including township, range, and section. (This is the Public Land Survey System—also known as PLSS—the current standard used to survey land in the United States. There are better alternatives, but we're likely stuck with this one for our lifetimes, so get used to it.)

Property address (if available): This is the street address format you use for your mail, such as 10 Main Street, Mosquito, FL 33500.

Plat map (if available): Shows where your property is located within a subdivision.

Survey map (if available): Shows the actual USGS (United States Geological Survey) map of the area.

The truth is, you often (especially in the Southwest) won't find anything beyond the property description. That's OK. Many properties are located in unincorporated areas, so they have no address or subdivision.

Not a problem. You can get this information from two websites.

"Wait, Mark. Hold up a sec here. Don't professional title companies usually handle all this detailed mumbo jumbo?"

Yes, they do. But when it comes to vacant land that is dirt cheap, most of the time the services of a title company aren't worth the investment.

My general rule (with exceptions) is if the property is $5,000 or more, I hire a professional title company. For $5,000 or less, I generally do the title research myself or outsource it to my virtual assistant. (Again, this is not legal advice; this is just what I do.)

If I were to spend the high fees for a professional title company, then I wouldn't make money on the vast majority of properties I sell. However, for larger deals where I sell on terms over a long period such as fifteen years, then I will definitely spend the money and get title insurance. If you were paying me $20,000 over a period of fifteen years for a forty-acre parcel, you'd want title insurance, right? Of course you would.

So you've verified the name on the deed and you know the title is clean. You have at least the legal description and the APN. Now what? Now you want to take a good hard look at the property.

"You mean I have to get on a plane and go there?"

Heck no! That's the beauty of this business. You can buy and sell land without ever having to see it or even be near it. You can live on an island in the Caribbean and work this business as long as you have a computer and internet connection.

What do I mean by a "good hard look at the property"?

A good hard *virtual* look.

Here are two of my favorite websites:

what3words.com
GoogleEarth.com

You're going to go to these sites and get all the information you need. If you have the property address (with township, range, and section), GPS coordinates, plat and survey maps, then Google Earth is fine. Plug in the address or township, range, and section, and you can take a virtual tour. (Isn't the twenty-first century amazing? Just twenty years ago, none of this was possible.)

If you have only the legal description, then What3Words.com will show you the rest. Type it in, and you will be amazed at the detail you see.

Take a look at the access. Is the property easy to get to? How far away is the road? Is there easement, meaning do you need to cross other people's properties to get to this one?

What kind of terrain is it—flat, hilly, rocky?

What type of soil—clay, sand, silt?

What type of environment—desert, deciduous, mountainous?

What covers the land—sawgrass, trees, dry lake bed?

"Mark, why on earth do I need to know all this?"

You do want to sell the property, don't you? When selling, chances are you will be asked questions about it, so it's good to know the answers. It's not the end of the world if you don't know everything, however, especially on an inexpensive parcel. Just tell your potential buyer, "I'm not sure. Let me call the county assessor or planning and zoning and get that information for you." Always be honest. Don't pretend to know something if you don't. The best thing you can do for your reputation is to always tell the truth.

If you have a large enough deal—forty acres, for example—then it's a good idea to hire someone to physically go to the location to stomp on it and take pictures. There is an amazing resource just for this:

Wegolook.com

They have independent contractors located throughout the country. For a fee, they will send out their local agent to verify whatever you need to know about the property. Plus, they'll take high-definition pictures and video for you to use in your marketing.

"Mark, all this is costing me money. Homeinfomax.com has

a membership fee. So does expertgps.com. Now you're telling me I need to spend more money at wegolook.com?"

Reality check: this is a business. You wouldn't open up a restaurant without buying some chairs and tables, right? The truth is, you're going to have to spend some money up front (but not a lot) to get your land business up and running. When you look at the return on your investment, these fees become minuscule by comparison.

There is one final step to due diligence: call the planning and zoning department of your county. You want to ask them:

What are the restrictions?

What is the water table?

What's allowed (RVs, mobile homes, hunting, camping)?

Now that you have determined that this is indeed a property you want to buy, it's time to buy it.

Let's close this deal!

Chapter 9

Deal! The Art of Closing

There are three basic ways to close a deal:

Direct

De facto notary

Simplifile

My favorite method, by far, is the first one. It's also the easiest.

I call up the seller on the phone and confirm the offer acceptance. Then I say, "Doug, I'm going to send you a deed to sign, notarize, and send back to me. Once we have it back, we'll record it and then send you a check. Deal?"

If Doug the seller says yes (which he will 90 percent of the time), then do just that: send him a deed, wait for it to come back signed and notarized, send it to the county for recording, wait for it to be recorded, and then send Doug a check.

Sometimes, however, the seller will say something like, "Whoa, wait a minute. You want me to just trust you to handle the entire process? How do I know you'll just take my property and never pay me?"

I respond by saying, "Doug, I've been buying and selling land since 2001. My company, Frontier Properties USA, is rated A+ by the Better Business Bureau and I have a long list of happy customers you can see on my website. Do you think it would be worth it to me, Doug, to rob you of $800 and risk my reputation like that?"

Usually that's enough, and the seller says OK. For you just starting out, you'll need a different response. You could say,

> Doug, I'm building a business based on trust. I'm eventually going to have a website with hundreds of testimonials from happy, satisfied customers. I understand you don't know me from a hole in the wall, and I get that. It's hard to trust people in today's world. I'll tell you what. I will take a video of me sending the

deed to the county recorder. Then I will take a video of me writing you a check and sending it in the mail. If I do this, Doug, and all goes the way I say it will, will you please record a video testimonial for me that I can use on my website?

This will usually clear up any issues or concerns the seller may have.

But as you likely know, there are some tough nuts to crack out there. Some people will insist that we go through a title company, which is just plain ridiculous because the cost of hiring a title company is often half the price of the property.

In a case like this, I just say, "Sure, that's fine. But if you want title insurance, you're going to have to pay for it."

When they discover the cost, they always say, "Hmm, maybe we won't go that route."

If they're still resistant, I will offer to send the check to a de facto notary who acts as escrow. I instruct the notary to hold on to the check until after the county records the deed.

"Mark, why do you wait until after the county records the deed?"

Because even with all the due diligence in the world,

sometimes I will miss something. The county may kick the deed back to me for a variety of reasons, sometimes odd, strange ones unique to that county.

It's usually no big deal. I just correct the information, resend the deed, and it gets recorded.

But you never know. Rarely, the deed comes back with a serious issue: the owner isn't really the owner, or perhaps there is a margin error on the deed which doesn't comply with the County Recorder's deed standards.

If I've sent the seller a check and the deed gets kicked back due to an error on his side, then I'm the one who could get screwed out of my money. The seller could easily vanish, retaining ownership of the property and my money.

Sure, I could sue, but that also would likely cost a lot more than the offer I sent to him. That is why it's just a safe-and-sound idea to wait for the deed to be properly recorded before sending the seller his money.

Nowadays, I go through Simplifile. This is an online service that securely records deeds via email. It's the fastest method. In some cases, the seller could have his money in twenty-four hours.

"Mark, where do I get a deed?"

Easy. As part of my Land Geek mentoring program, you get access to LGPASS, the proprietary Land Geek system that not only automates your mailings, but it also automates your deed processing.

Then you can go to this neat site:

Deeds.com

There, you can purchase deeds for anywhere in the United States. They will also include any other supporting paperwork required by certain states.

For example, in Arizona you need to fill out a form called an Affidavit of Property Value. Deeds.com includes this with the deed for any county in Arizona.

Or you could look at a pdf of the old deed and just copy it. How's that for economical? Just open up a Word document and mimic the font and spacing just how it was done on the previous one.

Now you've actually bought a property. Congratulations!

"Uh-oh, what do I do with it now?" you're thinking.

Time to sell it!

Chapter 10

How to Market Land

———

One of the best advances in the twenty-first century so far is the myriad of ways you are able to sell things. Land is no exception.

In fact, this business would not be possible if it weren't for websites that specialize in selling. It started with Amazon and eBay twenty years ago and now encompasses a variety of online stores, each with its own specialty.

I mean, come on. Name a store, and it has a website you can visit, click a few times, and get anything delivered to your door.

Yes, even land.

Like I mentioned before, there are a slew, a plethora

of land sites that do nothing but sell land all day long every day.

Who knew, right?

Yes, these are places where you can sell your land. Yes, you have to pay them; they're not doing it for free.

When I started, eBay was the most amazing place to sell land. I sold my first few parcels there, and I was hooked for life. Or so I thought.

Truth is, times change. I have no idea what year you're reading this book, but right now in 2018, eBay has fallen from its perch for land sales, which is not to say it won't rise again like a phoenix from the ashes.

But right now, the best place to market properties is—hmm, should I tell you? Oh wait, I already told you earlier—

The Neighbors and then...

Craigslist!

Yes, that Craigslist. The same one that hasn't modified its fonts since *Friends*, *Seinfeld*, and *ER* were must-see TV on Thursday nights.

"Mark, come on. You're not selling me on the idea that in today's world, Craigslist is the best place to sell land."

Fine, don't believe me.

Believe my friend Scott Todd, who recently sold 10 acres in Florida on Craigslist for $9,900, $1,000 down and $199/month. (He paid $890 for it.)

Or how about Tate Litchfield, who recently sold a 40-acre property in Oregon on Craigslist for $22,900, $3,000 down and $499/month. (He paid $5,000 for it.)

Don't want to believe that you can sell property on Craigslist for major dollars? Fine, then don't believe me. But it's true.

Now, don't get me wrong. I have had many amazing transactions through the "land sites" as well as through eBay. I'm not knocking them. They're all fantastic and provide a great service.

But from 2008 to now, Craigslist has been my go-to place. Maybe by the time the second edition of *Dirt Rich* has been published, this will have changed, but as of 2018, this is where we are.

So what makes Craigslist such a great place to sell land?

First, traffic. In the United States, Craigslist is still the go-to message board for buying and selling locally.

Second, Craigslist buyers are real buyers. Generally, most people who post or browse Craigslist ads are serious buyers or sellers. They're also bargain hunters, which fits nicely into our niche.

So no matter where you post your ad, you're going to need some basics in place. You already have pictures of the property, the legal description, the GPS coordinates, and all that you learned from the county assessor and the planning and zoning department.

Yes, it's good to list all that. You want to be transparent.

No, it's not enough to just list all that. You need to now think like an advertiser, because that's what you are. You have a business. Your inventory is land. You need to sell that land. No matter how wonderful that parcel of land is, you still need to employ some marketing techniques.

The Headline

For years, advertising copywriters have sung the praises of headlines and for good reason. Headlines grab our attention, triggering us to look at an ad.

I'm not going to repeat endlessly what others have written. There are countless books on writing ads such as *Tested Advertising Methods* by John Caples (with is possibly the best collection of headline generators ever), *Ca$hvertising* by Drew Eric Whitman, and *The Ultimate Sales Letter* by Dan Kennedy.

Sure, you can study those books and become a great copywriter or you could go to Fiverr and hire someone who has read all those books to write your Craigslist ads. If you want to build a dedicated team (which is an even better idea), go to Upwork.com and hire someone to write all your ads (because the truth is, you're going to need a lot of them, much more than you can ever imagine).

"Mark, hold up a sec. Craigslist allows you to post ads only one at a time in your own city. Why will I need so many ads?"

Ah, young Padawan, I like your thinking. The answer lies in the Force. Well, maybe not the actual Force, but as part of our coaching program at the Land Geek, we offer a program called, appropriately, Posting Domination, which is indeed Force-like. I can't go into details here, but check out the link:

http://www.postingdomination.com/thelandgeek

Therein lies your answers, young Jedi. Suffice it to say

that you will need a lot of ads, but you don't need to write them yourself.

Key words are an important element in your ads as well. You want to use as many of them in as many varied and different ways as possible. Here are some of my favorites:

Escape: "Escape the city to your own stunning five-acre private retreat!" Whom are we marketing to with this word? Stressed-out city people, outdoors enthusiasts, people who want to live off the grid, people who might want a second home.

Steal: "Steal this five-acre parcel before it's gone!" Whom are we talking directly to here? Bargain hunters, deal junkies, investors.

Path of growth: "Beautiful five-acre lot directly in the path of growth!" This is an important concept and marketing tool. I'm sure you've heard of people who own cheap land who are offered ten times the value of the property by a developer and suddenly retire.

It happens. It actually happens more often than you think.

Don't count on it, though. That's the age-old mistake land investors make: betting it all on speculation.

Just ask anyone who invested in Pahrump, Nevada, in the 1960s. Touted as the next Las Vegas, investors lined up to buy overpriced land destined for casinos and grand resorts.

While Pahrump did grow as a community, it never reached the destination status proffered by the developers. A lot of people lost a lot of money.

In land, as in any type of real estate, you just never know. Don't put all your eggs in one basket, and always do your due diligence.

Yes, it's quite possible that an area in which you buy is on the path of growth (and there are general indicators based on city and population growth), but you're better off just focusing on your M&Ms: mailing and marketing. Buy and sell. This is at heart a volume business.

Velocity is key. Buy often, sell often. Build up your note portfolio. Soon, you'll have grocery money, which becomes car payment money, which becomes mortgage money, which becomes retirement money.

So let's review. For marketing, you're going to advertise your property on:

Paper letters you send to the neighbors

Craigslist

Facebook Buy Sell Groups

Land sites (LandWatch, Land and Farm, etc.)

eBay (only if it doesn't sell for sixty to ninety days while on any of the other sites)

You're going to get phone calls and emails. The vast majority of them will be tire kickers or people who want to get information from you for a variety of purposes.

Stay focused. Selling can take a while. It should take only thirty days. If you did your comps right and marketed right, then that's the ideal time frame.

But if it doesn't sell in thirty days, you have several options:

Reduce your price

Make your terms more attractive (maybe drop the payments, the number of months, or your documentation fee)

List on eBay

That last one is my option of last resort nowadays. eBay

used to be good to me, but in recent years, it has become deluged with people who bid on a property and win but then never pay.

Your only option is to complain to eBay about it. They will investigate and return your closing fee of $35, but typically, you're stuck losing the original $35 (as of this writing) that it costs to place an ad.

That's not to say that property isn't bought and sold on eBay every day, all day long. It certainly is. Just beware of the pitfalls.

Another reason eBay is a place of last resort is that typically you generally sell for less. eBay buyers are notorious bargain hunters.

Chapter 11

It's All in Your Head

Why do some companies (and people, for that matter) succeed and why do others fail? In all the great companies, leaders think different. Stop for a second and absorb that.

Think different.

What company pops to mind with that phrase? Apple, right? That was their slogan for many years, but it was much more than a slogan; it was a powerful message to the world. Steve Jobs didn't just invent computers; he inspired a movement.

Jobs wasn't content with just inventing machines that do things. He really *did* think different. He envisioned a virtual army of creative-minded people who wanted to revolutionize the world.

Regardless of his flaws, Jobs had a solid purpose, a WHY that superseded processors, drives, and operating systems.

Let's look at another big name in technology. In the mid-1980s, Dell was on the road to dominating the computer market. Led by its charismatic founder Michael Dell, Dell started to appear as the PC of choice in businesses, universities, and government agencies.

Then something strange happened. Dell went from the next big thing to yesterday's news in a heartbeat. Startups such as Gateway, Acer, and Asus invaded the market and stole revenue from Dell. Toshiba and Hewlett-Packard launched successful offenses.

Dell soon found itself at the bottom of the barrel, bleeding and wounded by a barrage of negative customer reviews. Why? Many have made the case that Michael Dell was focused purely on money and profit. I can't say. I do not know Michael Dell, and I do admire the fact he was able to start a company and compete in the Wild West days of PCs and the birth of the internet.

But something went askew.

Now, don't get me wrong. There is nothing wrong with money. I'm not one of those anti-capitalism people who believe that making a boatload of money is a bad thing. Not at all. If you want to be a multimillionaire, fantastic!

But in order to sustain the levels of dedication and energy required to make large amounts of money, there needs to be a certain rocket fuel behind the endeavor. At first, it's enough to want the money, but eventually, you need something more to keep going.

Yes, big fancy yachts are nice. Yes, large homes with manicured lawns with a Mercedes parked out front are nice (although personally I don't need any of that anymore). But once you get those things, you tend to feel...

...meh.

I know this is hard to read if you're living paycheck to paycheck right now. I understand. I've been in both situations. I've lived on the edge of poverty, and I've also lived wealthy beyond my dreams.

But I learned the hard way that mansions and marble fountains are not the road to happiness. Happiness comes from three things: your relationships with others, your experiences, and your contributions.

The way I see it, Michael Dell accomplished his goals,

rich and successful beyond his wildest dreams. Then he was faced with a question:

"What now?"

His why wasn't big enough to outlast the requirements for the constant innovation required to stay at the top of the pack.

So back to Michael Dell. Brilliant and resourceful, he built a company worth billions. But overnight, like Austin Powers, he lost his mojo. He got into some legal trouble, was brutally knocked down in the marketplace, and was never able to recapture the momentum of his early days.

We can speculate all we want, but I believe the big difference between Michael Dell and Steve Jobs is that Dell's why was growing a company and making money, whereas Steve Jobs's why was changing the world.

Both succeeded. But notice that once Michael Dell got there, he floundered. Steve Jobs's why is still ongoing, even though its progenitor is no longer here.

Plenty of books have been written about thinking big. They're great, but they often miss the sublime purpose behind the reasons we do what we do.

Simon Sinek, in his amazing book *Start with Why*, introduces the idea that the why behind what we do is much more powerful than the what.

Why do some people succeed in land investing while others fail? For the same reason.

My friend and colleague Scott Todd bought my course on October 28, 2014, at 10:21 p.m. An executive at a major American corporation, he had just relocated to Orlando, Florida, to work at his company's headquarters.

The very month he arrived, Jim Cramer of the TV show *Mad Money* featured Scott's boss on his infamous Wall of Shame. Soon thereafter, Scott's company went through a period of turmoil. The CEO was ousted, and the executive team was outsourced, including Scott, who had bet the farm and moved to Florida.

Scott suddenly had a really big why to get involved in land investing: his wife and kids. Here he was in a new home, suddenly unemployed.

Scott's why was paramount: feed my family. Not only did Scott work day and night to build his land business, but he also became my top student and business partner.

What is *your* why?

The Two-Hour Workweek

I like to joke on podcast interviews that my next book should be *The 2-Hour Workweek*, sarcastically mocking the Tim Ferriss book, *The 4-Hour Workweek*.

The fact is, I do work "in" Frontier Properties about two hours a week simply managing our acquisition manager and the virtual assistants. Nevertheless, I work "on" the business constantly. *The E Myth* by Michael Gerber discusses in detail how most entrepreneurs build a job for themselves rather than a business that can operate without their involvement. I worked tirelessly for five years creating systems, automation, and delegation.

I have come to the stark realization that I have about eleven thousand days left on Earth according to the Chrome plug-in Death Clock. As a result, I am vicious with how I spend my limited days left on this blue spinning rock. I like to always say, "I can make more money, but I can't get more time." So I will literally invest any amount of money to save myself time.

In order for this book to remain relevant, I don't want to list all the software applications I use today to automate my business, as just in the past twelve months, so much of what I used to use has changed to better, less expensive options.

Simply put, between LGPASS, the Land Geek virtual assistants located in our office in the Philippines, and GeekPay. io, I have created a true machine that operates without my involvement. I want you to do the same.

If after reading this book you feel overwhelmed by all the moving parts, take a nice deep relaxing breath. Every pain point I have in this business has been solved by systems, delegation, and automation.

It is now time for you to adopt an entrepreneurial mindset.

An Entrepreneurial Mindset

Do you think Kevin Johnson, the CEO of Starbucks, is whipping up your Frappuccino in the morning? Of course not. He is working on the strategy and exploring new, potentially lucrative growth opportunities to maximize shareholder value. That's it. He is simply building something bigger than himself. In your land business, you are doing the same thing.

It all starts with the discipline to step back and create a system that is so clear, simple, and concise that anyone can execute it. I will create a system for my business and have my thirteen-year-old daughter read it, and if she doesn't understand something, then it's back to the drawing board until it's perfectly clear.

When this happens, you become bulletproof. You are not

vulnerable to a virtual assistant quitting or a key employee deciding they want to travel the world with a dude named Cole. The system is what remains, and the person executing it is secondary.

A must-read book for every entrepreneur is *Virtual Freedom* by Chris Ducker, as he outlines a step-by-step system to working with virtual assistants—how to hire them, what to pay them, and other critical issues to begin working with the best talent on the planet.

Remember to ask yourself every day when you are working "in" your land investing business and gaining confidence, "How can I remove this task forever?" Even if it takes you only five seconds to complete, that's five seconds you just saved forever. You are now freeing up your time to work on only the important areas of your business to drive growth such as marketing and sales.

My Favorite Word: *Automation*

There has never been in the history of business a better time to be alive. Software systems are so powerful and relatively inexpensive. What once took me twenty minutes a day to complete paperwork now takes literally two seconds (of course, I don't personally do the paperwork either anymore). If you aren't geeking out over automation systems on a daily basis and keeping up with the powerful, inexpensive programs that can run your business, you are missing out on huge time-saving opportunities. Please refer to www.thelandgeeek.com/dirtrich pdf to see the current software solutions we are implementing to automate our business.

Again, I don't want you to get bogged down in technology. I ran my land business for years using virtual assistants for my mailings and excel spreadsheets. That's it. It worked, but it certainly didn't promote any type of growth. I just hit a point of plateau and couldn't figure out why, until my first mentor, Ori, looked at my systems and scolded me for creating a job for myself.

I then started working at least an hour a day on stepping back, creating systems, and looking for automation tools to save time. I was a man possessed. Even today, I will try anything if it can possibly save me time and, even better, if it saves time and money.

From mailings to due diligence, to closing with your seller, to marketing, to closing with your buyer and managing the note, 90 percent of this business can be run with a few inexpensive virtual assistants and software.

There is no better feeling waking up to money in your account when you personally didn't have to expend any effort to make that money hit your account. It just was automatic because you took the time to build a true business and not a job for yourself.

Chapter 12

Avoiding the Biggest Mistake

———

I received an email from one of my coaching clients who was struggling. He had been working our program for three months and getting frustrated he wasn't seeing results. He started to doubt if the program would work for him. He wanted to know the all-important question: when do I quit?

I love watching *Shark Tank* with Mr. Wonderful Kevin O'Leary, an abrasive billionaire. He's kind of like the Simon Cowell of *Shark Tank*, not really caring about the feelings of the entrepreneur. He doesn't want them to waste their time on a business that just won't work out.

He sees flawed models all the time: the market is too small, the manufacturing is too expensive and there's not enough profit, they've been working at it for years and still can't break through due to competition, etc.

My answer to when to quit is this: thirty-six months. If in thirty-six months you have worked a focused two hours a day in land investing and it hasn't moved the needle in your life, move on. It's really and truly not for you.

Whether it's land investing or any other entrepreneurial venture, you need to have grit. You need patience, and you need to be kind to yourself. If you aren't enjoying the journey, that's good; it means you are uncomfortable. One of my favorite quotes is by Tim Ferriss, author of *The 4-Hour Workweek*: "A person's success in life can usually be measured by the number of uncomfortable conversations he or she is willing to have."

It takes grit to be uncomfortable and get knocked down again and again and still be determined to get better each day. If you are reading this book, I guarantee you have the grit to make our land investing model work for you.

When you combine a powerful "Why" along with the intellectual knowledge of escaping solo-economic dependency you have an unstoppable determination to fuel your life's purpose in ways you have yet to discover.

I have no passion for the raw land I acquire. I have passion for what this land investing business has provided for myself, my family and my clients. Financial security, freedom and flexibility of how to manage my days. It has provided time for me to focus on what really makes me truly happy. The quality of my relationships, helping others and growing personally and professionally.

The sad truth is most people won't ever accomplish their dream of total financial and time freedom. They will get derailed by obstacles real or imagined. They will make excuses and move on to the next hot make money trend.

If you don't want to be one of those people, now is the time to commit to those 36 months of daily effort and kaizen. Of course, we can be your sherpa up the mountain of land investing success and help you get there more quickly and safely, but it will still be an arduous exhilarating climb. My advice is don't go it alone. If you don't want the Land Geek community to be your mentor on your climb, no worries. But, find someone whom has already accomplished what you want to accomplish and simply follow their footsteps. No reason to re-invent the wheel and suffer just to suffer.

I wish you well on your journey and I'm so grateful that you took the time to learn more and explore what I consider the best passive income model. Feel free to email me directly if this book has made any type of impact on you. My email is mark@thelandgeek.com.

To close, I think Zig Ziglar the motivational speaker said it so eloquently: "If you'll do for the next three to five years what other people won't do, you'll be able to do for the rest of your life what other people can't do."

Thanks for reading this book.

To engineering your success,

MARK

Additional Resources

———

Learn more at www.thelandgeek.com.

Resources: www.thelandgeek.com/dirtrich

Free Facebook Group: The Official Land Geek Wealth & Motivation Group

Acknowledgments

———

When I first thought about writing a book about my story and land investing, I was filled with doubt and fear. I thought, "Who do you think you are to write a book? Why would anyone read your story or take your advice?" Then I thought about my children and how I could be a role model for them. So I thought, "Why not me? I've accomplished some cool stuff." Nevertheless, I think it takes a certain amount of hubris to put your thoughts in hundreds of pages and think you actually know something well enough that you should share it with people. That being said, if not for the following people, I would have never written this book, and now it's up to you, the reader, to let me know if this was folly or not.

If not for the following people, I can tell you life would be like living in an old black-and-white TV show instead of color. All of the following people have had such a positive impact on me and the creation of this book. My gratitude for you has no limits.

First, I am thrilled to thank my beautiful, talented, and hilarious wife, Rachel—marrying her has been my best decision in so many ways. Through twenty years of ups and downs, she has weathered it all in good humor and understanding. She is the best wife, mother, and friend that I know. Her unwavering support has allowed me to grow in ways I didn't even know were possible. She is my rock, and I feel blessed every day to wake up to her smiling face. Boo, I truly love spending this life with you and feel so blessed and humbled by it all.

My three children, Noah, Elan, and Ella, are my big "Why." The three of you teach me every day about the power of curiosity, patience, and priority. Even though I annoy each of you on a daily basis, it is my way of trying, albeit awkwardly, to connect with you. You teach me about humility, uncertainty, and unconditional love. I am so proud of the people you are and can't wait to see the contribution you make in this world. You three inspire me daily.

The Land Geek team comprised of Scott Todd, Tate Litchfield, Mike Zaino, Scott Bossman, Erik Peterson, and Danielle Clark DyBall is truly extraordinary. We are a small bunch, but each of you work so hard to help others accomplish their respective dreams, and it's truly a joy to work with you every day. All of you have contributed so much individually in so many ways, from Danielle running the show (which is a nice way of saying doing just about everything LG related), to Erik helping with the cover on this book and providing so much advice, and Scott Todd just being the personification of what one person can accomplish in this business when they focus and "move their feet." Tate, Frontier Properties continues to thrive because of all your tireless efforts, and I'm so grateful. Plus, you are the best land-investing coach combining passion with encouragement in a way I wish I could bottle and drink every day. Mike "Zen Master" Zaino, you have been such a calming force to the community in so many ways, and I'm so appreciative of all your hard work. You are pure gold. And, of course, Scott Bossman, you have been a pleasure to watch grow from client to coach, and I'm so proud of your accomplishments. My gratitude for all of you is so deep and profound, and I know I don't say thank you enough to all of you, but please know that I am so thankful and appreciative.

The Land Geek community is thriving and growing. From every coaching client, Flight School client, and investor's toolkit owner, I am so humbled and privileged that you allow us to help you achieve your passive income goals. Thank you for all your support and feedback to help us improve and grow. I love meeting all of you at our quarterly boot camps and seeing in person how amazingly smart and talented our community is at those events.

I have many mentors and friends to thank—too many really—and I'm deeply fearful of leaving anyone out and hurting someone's feelings. As a result, if you are reading this, then you know I include you and I thank you for all your support and encouragement throughout the years.

I want to thank the talented people at Lioncrest Publishing—especially Julie Arends for keeping me calm during the entire process and being there for me every step of the way.

As a first-time author, this was a fantastic experience.

As I end each podcast, "Let freedom ring..."

About the Author

 Armed with $3,000 and no real estate experience, MARK PODOLSKY bought his first parcels of land in 2001. Now, he is the owner of Frontier Properties, a successful investing company, and has completed more than five thousand lucrative land deals. He is also the founder of geekpay.io, an automated collection system that helps lenders get payments from borrowers without collection headaches.

Having escaped the corporate world and solo-economic dependency himself, Mark works as a coach and mentor to help others achieve their financial freedom goals. He is dedicated to teaching current, relevant, "real-world" investing methods to his students.